Doing What's Right

Doing
What's
Right

HOW TO FIGHT FOR WHAT YOU

BELIEVE—AND MAKE A DIFFERENCE

Tavis Smiley

Doubleday

New York   London   Toronto   Sydney   Auckland

PUBLISHED BY DOUBLEDAY

a division of Random House, Inc.

1540 Broadway, New York, New York 10036

DOUBLEDAY and the portrayal of an anchor with a dolphin are trademarks
of Doubleday, a division of Random House, Inc.

Book design by Chris Welch

Library of Congress Cataloging-in-Publication Data

Smiley, Tavis, 1964–
Doing what's right : how to fight for what you believe—and make a
difference Tavis Smiley.— 1st ed.
p.   cm.
Includes index.
1. Responsibility.   2. Conduct of life.   3. Social change.   I. Title.
BJ1451 .S66   2000
170′.44—dc21
99-050205

ISBN 0-385-49930-2

1   3   5   7   9   10   8   6   4   2

For

Tom Bradley

"Big George" Hughley

&

Daisy M. "Big Mama" Robinson

Acknowledgments

Every time I hear someone refer to me as an author, I twinge. Not because I have anything against writers, but I guess first and foremost I see myself as an advocate. I actually have an immense amount of respect for authors; because of all the things I do (television, radio, and lectures), writing challenges me the most.

Fortunately, I have been blessed to be surrounded by good folk who have helped me meet the challenge for a fourth time now. In previous books, I've had occasion to thank all of my family and friends. Your love keeps lifting me higher.

I do, however, need to thank the only editor I have ever

had or hope to work with, Roger Scholl; his able assistant, Stephanie Rosenfeld, and the publisher of Doubleday, Steve Rubin, for embracing and agreeing to distribute my work.

The invaluable contribution of Sonya Ross has made this a book I am more than proud of. Thank you, Sonya!

People often ask me why I still fly between Los Angeles and Washington every week, as I have been for the past four years. Wouldn't it be easier just to live in Washington, where the show usually originates from, they ask. My response is simple. I return to LA weekly for the spiritual guidance and intellectual stimulation that I receive from my pastor, Bishop Noel Jones. Nobody does it better.

Finally, the people who represent me so well every day: Ken Browning, Wendi Chavis, Errol Collier, Kathye Davenport, Dawn Fong, Kimberly Tolbert, and my abiding friends Harold W. Patrick and Denise Pines.

Contents

Doing
What's
Right

Why We Need Advocates

To let the politicians and the social indicators tell it, these are absolutely the best of times in the United States, the most prosperous society in the world. The economy is booming. Jobs abound. Crime is down. Unemployment is at a thirty-year low, the Dow is at an all-time high. More Americans own their own homes than ever before. Other factors that speak to quality of life—college enrollment, birthrates, salaries, consumer purchases—are also on the upswing.

But beneath these good vibes and good times lies a dark

underbelly of despair, for America's problems are more serious than we want to believe. Our economy is booming, but a number of countries in Asia, Eastern Europe, and South America have had serious problems which could eventually hit home with us. Jobs are abundant, but the majority of them either require advanced technical skills or are service-industry positions that barely pay a livable wage—hardly a choice for unskilled people who are leaving the welfare rolls to join the workforce. We are not certain that Social Security or Medicare will survive long enough to take care of the huge baby boom generation. Crime is down, but violent crime is up, especially among juveniles, and the United States has the highest rate of incarceration in the world, basically rendering the jailed useless to the rest of society. Blacks and Hispanics remain less likely than whites to secure a home mortgage. And the Dow is hardly a barometer for measuring the heartbreak of those who are wondering where their next meal is coming from.

We can continue to ignore these unsolved problems, or pay short shrift to them, but if we do, they will remain with us well into the new millennium. They will worsen and foster an environment for new problems, creating a burden for our children and grandchildren.

We had heady prosperity during the 1980s too. But we

chose to live for the day. We ran up huge debts on our credit cards, financed ourselves to the hilt, and got in way over our heads. We ran up huge debt on the *nation's* credit cards as well, creating massive federal budget deficits that were creeping toward the trillions of dollars. Then we crashed and burned. We ended the eighties in a recession. Now, ten years later, things are good again. But we may be setting ourselves up for another crash-and-burn. Indeed, as I write this book, President Bill Clinton and the Republicans are at war over what to do with a federal budget surplus. The Republicans were pushing a plan to cut taxes by billions of dollars, while the president argued that the GOP tax cut would rob safety-net social programs of much-needed cash.

Right now, America is experiencing an erosion of values in its communities. There is an increasing sense of isolation in neighborhoods, as more of us simply pass through on our way from one city to the next and fewer of us truly get to know the family next door. Militia groups attack our government as an entity; indeed they work to destroy our government. They don't value patriotism as we know it— they think they are being patriotic by rejecting, in the name of constitutionally protected personal freedoms, everything the United States stands for. We watched millions of people die in Rwanda and Bosnia and did virtually nothing to stop those slaughters. Instead, we debated whether we needed to get involved in such conflicts because the United States can't police the world. Increasingly, holding elective office has become more about raising money than raising issues, where serving private interests becomes more important than serving the public good. We used to greet new neighbors with fresh-baked pies. Today we greet them with laws that demand disclosure of whether they are sex offenders. All of these things converge to turn the Internet, a concept that was meant to revolutionize our society, into an arena that offers up some of the worst around us: hatespeak, child pornography, sedition. We want the advances the Internet and its associated technology bring, but the Internet also exposes some of the excesses that have become so much a part of our society.

As people take up arms in anger, neither our workplaces nor our homes—as evidenced by the rise in domestic shootings—offer protection. Not even our schools and churches are safe. The rise in violence in our streets has become so commonplace that people have grown inured to it, until it takes place in their own backyards.

Even the most jaded, however, were jolted by the killing spree in Littleton, Colorado, when two teenaged boys mowed down twelve of their high school classmates. It prompted all of us to question the level of violence we

....

subject our children to through movies and television, and video games that allow them to kill, hit the reset button, and kill again.

Three months later we were jolted again, when stock trader Mark O. Barton murdered his family and nine colleagues in Atlanta before killing himself.

While values were eroding and these events began to unfold, we also experienced a fundamental loss of trust and integrity. This loss is especially felt when it comes to our elected officials. During the nineties, hardly a day went by without word of some public official falling from grace. We saw President Clinton, a married man, impeached and later acquitted for having a young female intern perform sex acts on him in the Oval Office. We saw the president's cabinet secretaries—Bruce Babbitt, Ron Brown, Henry Cisneros, Hazel O'Leary, to name a few—paraded before grand juries and judges courtesy of investigations that never seemed to end. We saw Marion Barry, mayor of the nation's capital, led out of a hotel in handcuffs after smoking crack cocaine with a female friend (who was cooperating with authorities), complaining, "The b——— set me up." Later we saw Barry go to jail, then come out and get elected to his old job again. We saw a Speaker of the House of Representatives, Newt Gingrich, brought up on ethics charges. Gingrich's would-be successor, Representative Bob Livingston (R-La.), was forced to resign from office before he could ever wield the Speaker's gavel because of allegations that Livingston had had an extramarital affair. Months after he left the House, we learned Gingrich, too, had a three-year extramarital affair with a female Capitol Hill aide.

The guilt or innocence of these folks is not the issue. The fact is that we no longer trust our leaders and politicians. It has cast a pall over the many politicians doing the right things, who are working for the good of society.

Even our religious leaders have not been immune from scandal. The Reverend Henry Lyons, former head of the National Baptist Convention and pastor of a respected church in St. Petersburg, Florida, was discovered to have used his denomination's money to buy houses and expensive gifts for women associates, a scam uncovered when his wife set one house afire in a jealous rage. A minister in Virginia was arrested for trying to hire a hit man to kill his wife, and the Reverend Donald Moomaw, former pastor for President Ronald Reagan, was removed from the helm of his church for affairs with numerous women. The disillusion such leaders create has led some to the sense that there is no one to believe in anymore.

Our very icons and heroes have been brought crashing to earth. We found out that Martin Luther King, Jr., had affairs with women. More lurid and salacious details about John F. Kennedy and his brother Robert seem to surface almost daily. Respected sports announcer Marv Albert was accused of sexual assault and forced to resign his position in disgrace, only to surface two years later as an announcer for Madison Square Garden. Even Charles Kuralt, the trusted veteran CBS correspondent, we learned, led a double life, maintaining two families: one with his wife, the other with a longtime mistress.

This is only the tip of the iceberg. These stories have unfolded against a backdrop of crumbling communities, police brutality, racial tension, family breakdown, and moral erosion. These are clear indications that America, despite its unparalleled financial wealth, is nowhere near completing the work it must do to achieve an equal and just society.

Moreover, we are experiencing a seismic shift in our country's racial and ethnic composition. Projections are that by the year 2050 no single race will be the majority in this country. Like it or not, this new America will challenge us to live up to the nation's purported status as a melting pot. This should be easy stuff, but it's not. There are folks out there like Dinesh D'Souza and Ward Connerly postulating ideas about a united, color-blind America with one set of values, while others see what they are doing as undermining the very diversity that fosters such unity.

Congress can't even resolve as simple an issue as the 2000 census. Some want to use a sampling technique that would make the count more accurate than the 1990 census, which overlooked a significant number of people of color. Others reject that, arguing for a literal head count as the law stipulates, despite the fact that minorities, for a number of reasons, end up being glaringly undercounted.

But guess what, people? All of these problems exist because we created them through transgressions of commission and omission. But I believe that, just as we have created these problems, we can undo them. We can solve them. We have to begin to act consciously and deliberately toward creating a society in which we want to live. Sometimes this means having to stir things up. Sometimes it means having to advocate, to stand up for and fight for what we believe in.

We have gone too far, spent too much, and stayed too long at the party. Now we find ourselves in a nation gone awry. There are still too many people who are homeless, too many unemployed, hungry, or desperate. There is still too much violence, too little child care, health care, quality education. But it doesn't have to be that way. We don't have to simply accept things the way they are. We can make a difference and reshape our lives, our communities, our nation. It's never too late to get back to basics, to get back on course.

Truth be told, we're not doing the things we know we ought to be doing to preserve our society. We're not voting. We're not participating in the process. We're not help-ing each other the way we should. We barely know our neighbors. Let's not squander this great thing called America that our forebears gave us. We have to get out there and take up the reins of our communities and our lives. There is work to do—and only we can do it.

2

How I Did It

Let me share with you the story of how I became an advocate. I'm sharing my story because too often our problems seem larger than life, so much so that we think we can't make a difference. We don't know where to begin. Because we see the problems as so big, we think they require a larger-than-life solution as well. The fact is, no problem is too intractable or too overwhelming that it can't be addressed. We simply need to pick up the reins and begin.

What made John F. Kennedy, Robert F. Kennedy, and

Martin Luther King, Jr., so special is that through their leadership they inspired all of us to believe we, too, could make a difference. "Ask not what your country can do for you; ask what you can do for your country," John F. Kennedy exhorted us in his inaugural address. Martin Luther King said, "Anybody can be great, because anybody can serve. All it takes is a heart full of grace, a soul generated by love."

The great children's advocate Marian Wright Edelman once said, "Service is the price we pay for the space we occupy." It is the act of fighting for a cause in which you believe, feeling that through your efforts you are making a contribution. It's your way to be in service to people; ultimately, your cause becomes your contribution.

On any given day, a particular athlete can turn in a stellar performance that shows what an individual can do when we put forth our best effort. What made Michael Jordan so great is that he decided he was going to be the best in the game before picking up a basketball. He always gave his best effort, even when he was injured or he wasn't feeling well. In doing so, he inspired a whole generation of children to "be like Mike." Some of those children—the Grant Hills and Kobi Bryants of the world—came along to play beside him, freely acknowledging that he had set the example.

I was thirteen years old when I found the person who

....

set such an example for me. Douglas Hogan, one of the members of the city council in Kokomo, Indiana, was a member of my church, New Bethel Tabernacle. People were always coming up to him with different issues that needed to be addressed in the community. I saw the pride he took, the absolute joy he seemed to feel, in being able to respond to people's concerns and advocate on their behalf at city council meetings. Councilman Hogan was the Sunday school superintendent at New Bethel, and every so often, he would have a student lead the Sunday school discussion. One day he approached me about it, making me a Sunday school teacher at age thirteen.

Some time later, Senator Birch Bayh came to Kokomo for a campaign swing. As I heard him articulate why he was running for reelection, I saw Senator Bayh's determination and dedication toward making a difference. I was, at age thirteen, sandwiched between one guy who was making a difference on the local level and another guy who was making a difference on the national level. Listening to them talk, I soaked up their conversation like a sponge.

As a result, I became a volunteer in Bayh's unsuccessful campaign against Dan Quayle. I remained in contact with Bayh long after the campaign and continued to work with Councilman Hogan. I was curious how he was able to deliver on the things people demanded of him, and make their lives better. I didn't know anything about Kokomo's electoral hierarchy or how the process worked. What intrigued me was seeing Councilman Hogan respond to people's needs. Lucky for me, Hogan took an interest and spent some time with me. I rode along in the car as he drove around his district, talking to constituents about their issues and concerns. I would sit in his house and go through the mail. Councilman Hogan paid attention to me, something that a kid in a large family can't get all the time. I was at an age where I was open to learning and growth, and I was soaking up everything he had to offer, seeing how things got done.

Now, my parents were God-fearing people. The answer to everything was God. What I learned through hanging out with Councilman Hogan was that God doesn't come down from heaven to fill potholes. We've got to do that ourselves. I grew up with nine brothers and sisters. We had very little money. We were disenfranchised socially, politically, and economically, so I knew what it meant to go without. I remember vowing to God that if I ever had a chance to get out of that predicament, I would spend the rest of my life trying to do what Hogan was doing, helping make things better. If Douglas Hogan could earn the respect of the community and bring happiness to other people, I could too.

As a young child, my dream was to become a first baseman in the major leagues. After meeting Douglas Hogan,

....

I redirected my energies from sports to my academics. I started educating myself on political issues. My whole outlook changed.

After that, I became Mr. High School—National Honor Society, student council, speech team, class president from my sophomore year on, voted most likely to succeed. And this was at a predominantly white high school with only twenty-six black students. At the time I met Councilman Hogan, I didn't even know the word "advocacy." But by high school I was beginning to practice it.

For example, as a senior, I realized we'd never had an award to honor students for their civic work in the community. As class president, I lobbied for our class to give such an award. We had to petition our adviser and the principal, and I lobbied hard and won. I also felt it was important to encourage students to take pride in their respective classes. So we created "class competitions" in sports, in the arts. Each class had to compete over the course of a week. The intent was to build school spirit. It wasn't a complete success, but it was a start in the right direction.

In the fall of 1982 I went on to Indiana University, Bloomington, where I enrolled in the School of Public and Environmental Affairs. My concentration was Law and Public Policy. Asking myself, "How can I make a difference?," I joined the student advisory board at Read Hall; the purpose of the board was to lobby the Dorm Authority on behalf of the students to make dorm life better. We had fierce debates about quiet hours, about parties and alcohol, about the food, about how we dealt with students who got into trouble.

I was catapulted into social advocacy through a tragedy involving a friend of mine named Denver Smith. Denver was on the football team, married with a new baby. In my sophomore year Denver was murdered, as far as I was concerned, by the cops in Bloomington, Indiana. They said he was acting crazy, as if he was on PCP. They shot him an inordinate number of times in attempting to arrest him; half of the bullets hit Denver in the back. That's what made the story such a hot topic: a black college student killed by a bunch of white cops, seemingly for no reason. In Kokomo we didn't have those kinds of issues. We had potholes. That marked my first foray into the realm of social advocacy. For the first time in my life, I was out there on the cutting edge of a real-life issue, helping to lead protests, marching, holding rallies, speaking before the city council, conducting television interviews.

Sadly, our efforts in the Denver Smith tragedy yielded few tangible results. That's how it is with advocacy sometimes. It did make the Bloomington police department

....

take a hard look at how they would deal with such situations in the future, and it did unite a massive number of students, particularly black students, on campus. More than a few of us realized that unfair things happen because the world isn't fair, and that they would continue to happen unless we did something about them.

My involvement with the Denver Smith situation brought me to the attention of Bloomington's mayor, Tomilea Allison. She offered me an internship, a position that took me from the outside to the inside. Mayor Allison put me in charge of something called the Bloomington Community Progress Council, where I was to be an advocate for small business owners, finding ways to make the city more friendly.

In my senior year of college, I was ready to drop out of school. My parents were getting divorced. I felt burned-out on college, and I'd turned into a kid who thought he knew everything. Why did I need a college degree? A dear friend of mine, George Hughley, convinced me not to drop out. "If you need to take a semester off, do it. But get an internship. Get some matriculation credit," he said.

George lived in Los Angeles and once worked for Mayor Tom Bradley. He helped me land an internship with Bradley's office. The bad news was it was an *unpaid* internship. But hey, sometimes good advocates have to be willing to do what's necessary to get where they want to go. So I had to figure out how to survive in Los Angeles for an entire semester. I raised more than $4,000 from various members of the Bloomington Community Progress Council and, along with a little money I'd saved from my work-study job, bought a new set of tires, packed up my car, and rolled to California.

In Los Angeles, Mayor Bradley's staff wanted me to push paper and pens and open mail. I told the mayor, "Mr. Bradley, I know my internship is free, but I didn't come all the way to California to do this." As a result of speaking up, I was put by the mayor on two projects. The first involved working in the mayor's Office of Youth Development, the office that trained young people to be effective advocates in their communities.

The second occurred during the second half of my internship, when I became the mayor's point person for the Martin Luther King holiday. The coming January would mark the first year the city of Los Angeles would honor the holiday for King. My job was to organize the city's celebration in conjunction with the Southern Christian Leadership Conference of Greater Los Angeles. Together, we created quite an event, for the keynote speaker we were able to corral was Desmond Tutu, the

South African Anglican archbishop and Nobel Peace Prize winner.

When my four-month internship was over, I went back to school to finish up my education.

I had learned so much from Tom Bradley's office, I wanted to continue my work there, where I thought I could make the greatest impact, so in January 1987 I moved to Los Angeles. Mayor Bradley had offered me a job as one of his aides, but when I arrived in L.A., there was a hiring freeze. As a result, I had to go from the inside to the outside again. I took a job at the Los Angeles branch of the Southern Christian Leadership Conference, which was Martin Luther King's civil rights group, and found myself working at the grassroots level. We dealt with all kinds of issues: criminal justice, injustice, lack of affordable homes and home loans, the education crisis. Eventually, the hiring freeze lifted and I went back to working for Mayor Bradley.

Bradley had "area coordinators" who basically served as the mayor's eyes and ears in six Los Angeles communities. My area was South-Central, an area inhabited mostly by blacks and Hispanics—an area known to many as the place where the riots broke out. Every major bank was closing branches in that part of the city, and liquor stores were sprouting like weeds. There were no first-rate grocery stores. No movie theaters for entertainment. The insurance redlining issues were still hot. There was a lack of city services. I mean, we were trying to kick off a recycling program in the city and the black folks in South-Central didn't have bins.

After a few years I left the mayor's office to run for city council so I could help change things. I ran because the lady who was our city councilwoman at the time was not doing an effective job, and I thought I could do a better one. Unfortunately, I missed forcing her into a runoff by *thaaat much,* as Maxwell Smart would say. Although I lost, I got enough votes to realize there were a whole lot of people listening to what I was saying on the campaign trail and agreeing with me. That's the point. When you get out there and start raising your voice, letting your views and opinions be heard, you find there are folk out there who agree with you, who can become your compatriots and comrades in whatever your struggle is.

In the course of the campaign, I discovered there was no person of color on radio or television in Los Angeles who was doing political or social commentary. There was no one on the scene. And I realized that if I wanted to run again and win the next time, I needed a platform to continue to advocate for my views. Sometimes you have to create your own vehicles, you have to build your own platforms. Sometimes you've got to invent your own bully pulpit.

So that's what I did.

I created a little one-minute commentary called "The Smiley Report," and I went to the owner of KGFJ, a small AM station in Los Angeles, in October 1991. He told me, "Black is beautiful, but business is business. I love your little commentary, but you've got to find some money to buy this time." I went around, raised some money from former campaign supporters who believed in me and what I wanted to do. After that money ran out, one of the local banks stepped in. That's how I survived for about nine months on the radio. "The Smiley Report" ran every morning at 7:20—and it quickly became so popular the station aired it again at 5:20 in the afternoon. So there I was at age twenty-six, reaching out to listeners in morning and evening drive time, Monday through Friday. Eventually, I worked my way up from that small station to the largest FM urban station in the market, KKBT. In between, I worked for KJLH, owned by Stevie Wonder.

As people started calling the station asking for copies of my commentaries, *I realized one could arguably have more influence on the outside than on the inside, particularly when advocacy meets media. That is combustible. But with or without media, I realized it is the advocates who get the folks on the inside to do something.*

....

Fighting for what you believe in is the spark that lights a fire under the folks on the inside. Someone once told me advocates are like cooks. You don't always see them, but they are crucial to fixing a meal.

I'd just realized the power of media.

I went from airing my commentaries on KKBT to doing commentary during the 5 p.m. news on the ABC-TV affiliate in Los Angeles. Then the ABC talk radio station in Los Angeles called me. At one point, I was doing all three of them together—the urban station, the TV station, and talk radio on ABC. ABC offered me my own talk show, 9 P.M. till midnight. Then things began to snowball. I was featured in a cover story in *Time* magazine. I wrote a book called *Hard Left*, which was well received. I started doing commentaries on Tom Joyner's radio show, reaching out to some 7 million people, and in late 1996 I became host of my own show on Black Entertainment Television. I never auditioned for any of this stuff. I started like everybody else, and only got to where I am because others started to take note of what I was doing.

It was Bill Clinton who introduced me to Tom Joyner at a private White House reception in 1996. After reading my book *Hard Left,* Tom invited me to come onto his show to talk about the book. Afterward, Tom said, "I've got an idea. I'd like you to be part of my radio show. I'd like to make a difference in the 1996 elections." He had a

....

wacky, crazy idea of getting black folks to vote by *giving away a fully loaded Lexus, gold rims, gold kit, and all*. I told him our audience did not need to be bribed to vote. They needed to be educated. I suggested that what we needed was an old-fashioned voter registration campaign over the radio. I told him I could come on every day to do a commentary on why this '96 campaign was so important, and urge people to register to vote.

Our efforts worked beyond our wildest dreams. We blew out the switchboard at 1-800-REGISTER. Between July and October of 1996, we registered roughly a quarter million people. I called it "air advocacy." I tried to break down how the issues mattered. How politics touches every aspect of our lives. Politics, as Ron Brown used to say, is not a spectator sport. You've got to get off the sidelines and get in the game. I wanted listeners to see, as Big Mama said, "You can't win it if you ain't in it"—that we control our own destiny, but only to the extent that we're involved. Over and over again I shared that message and tried to explain the issues and the impact.

The approach was so successful that we decided to test it in another area the following year. In the fall of 1997 we learned that Fox Television was canceling the number one and number two television programs watched by black Americans, *Living Single* and *New York Undercover*. I was

....

particularly bothered because Fox, like so many networks, had used black viewers to get up on its feet. Somebody once said black folks are like starter kits for these networks. They use us to get their ratings established; then they switch the programming, dropping the black shows. I never liked the idea of these black nights anyway, where they lump all the black shows together.

I went on the radio and talked about this ad nauseam. I gave out the phone number and fax number for Peter Roth, who was then president of the Fox network. Finally one day Peter Roth had enough. He invited me to a meeting in his office. A few days later he announced that he was going to bring *Living Single* back on to start the fall season. Moreover, he came on Tom's show and apologized. Of course, *Living Single* didn't stay on the air. But to my knowledge, it was the first time in the history of television that a black show was brought back because of protests by its viewers.

We also discovered we have the power to cancel shows that offend us before they get up and running. We heard that UPN was planning a *sitcom* about slavery called *The Secret Diary of Desmond Pfeiffer*. My reaction was, what's so funny about slavery? I went on the air and listed the names of sponsors who bought advertising time for the show. One by one, the sponsors started dropping.

....

My next major advocacy campaign involved Christie's auction house. I found out on a Monday night that Christie's was set to auction off slave artifacts. Christie's had a policy of not auctioning off items from the Holocaust, yet they felt free to auction off artifacts from African enslavement as if there was some statute of limitations on black pain. I did my commentary on Tuesday morning. The auction was set for Wednesday morning. My fear was I couldn't mobilize our listeners in twenty-four hours. But as Tom said, "You've got to do it because it's the right thing to do." Ninety minutes after I came off the air that Tuesday, the president of Christie's called and said, "Stop the calls, stop the faxes!" Our efforts had shut down their entire system. I asked Christie's to do three things. One, take the items off the auction block. Two, donate them to a museum or historical society. Three, change their house policy regarding slave artifacts. They agreed on each count. They donated the artifacts to a black museum in Cincinnati, the Underground Railroad Museum, a $50-million project on the Ohio River which is set to open in the year 2003.

Even as I paused to catch my breath, I became immersed in the Katz Media imbroglio. It had to do with a racist memo written at a major advertising firm. The memo dealt with advertising and how to reach minority audiences without having to advertise to them. It was written by a Katz executive, instructing their clientele not to buy on black or Hispanic radio stations. "You want prospects, not suspects," the memo said. It was full of racist jargon. We went ballistic.

We challenged Stu Olds, president of Katz Media Group, who came on the radio program and apologized. But I wasn't satisfied. Once again, I gave out the phone number, fax number, and e-mail address for Katz to our listeners. In the end, we got Katz to do a number of things. They increased the number of blacks on their sales staff by 400 percent (before you get too excited, that raised the number from one to four). They started an internship program at two historically black colleges. We made them hire a firm to do diversity training. We had them double the rate of spending for black radio. They had to put together a list of twenty major companies that at the time did not do business with black media, and the president of the company committed himself to go to meetings with his sales staff to call on these companies to convince them they should do business with black media. A year later we tracked Katz's progress, and they had made some strides— good strides—in turning that situation around.

The day that I did my commentary and shut down their system, I'm told that Leslie Stahl of *60 Minutes* happened

....

to be in the Katz office. She was astounded by how effective we were. As a result, Stahl did an in-depth piece for *60 Minutes* on the power of black advocacy.

But again, you don't have to be on television or the radio to fight for what's right, or advocate change. When I worked for Tom Bradley, I organized a group called L.A.'s Young Black Professionals. I wanted to challenge black professionals to be advocates, to answer what Martin Luther King called life's most persistent and urgent question: What are you doing for others? We set up mentoring and tutoring programs for kids. We got involved on the political front by doing fund-raisers for candidates with whom we agreed politically. As a result, we received the 1990 Census Bureau's highest award for volunteerism. Ten years later the group is still going strong.

If I haven't convinced you of the power of advocacy yet, consider this: We can only make a difference if we get involved. And we've got to start somewhere. Let it begin with you. The fact is there are three types of people in the world: those who talk about what ought to be done, those who do what needs to be done, and folks who "playa hate," or denigrate when something is done. Be a doer.

While I don't mean to be preachy, what better example of somebody determined to help others than Jesus? Jesus once gave three men talents according to each man's abilities. The first man was given five, the second was given two, the third received one. They were told to take their gifts and do something worthwhile with them.

At the appointed time, all three men came back to give Jesus an account of what they had done with their gifts. The first one told Jesus, "You gave me five gifts, I've accomplished good things with them." He received five more talents. The second one did the same and received two additional talents. The last, however, hadn't done anything with the talent he was given. He dug a hole in the earth and hid his talent. Jesus was understandably disappointed and cast him away. He took the wasted talent and gave it to the man who now had ten.

One of the reasons I love this story is that there are any number of lessons to be drawn from it regarding advocacy:

1. Everyone is blessed with talent. No one comes into the world without unique gifts to do something special with. What you do with it is a whole 'nother question. But we have to get people to realize they have talents, they have gifts; they need only to discover them, define them, develop them. The talent is already there.

2. Each of our talents is on loan from God. It ain't ours to make unilateral decisions with. Rush Limbaugh uses

that line all the time, calling himself "talent on loan from God." The truth is he's right about the talent part. The use of his talent is open to debate.

3. If we don't use our talents, we will lose them. The last man in the parable did nothing with the talent Jesus gave him, and in the end he lost it.

4. We've all been blessed in uniquely different ways. Big Mama used to say there are twenty-four hours in the day—twelve hours to mind your business, twelve hours to leave other people's business alone. There are a variety of ways in which our talents and gifts can work if we let them, at the same time leaving others free to let their talents work for them.

5. If you use the gift or the talent God gave you to make a difference in the community, other opportunities will open for you to be of greater service. I never studied telecommunications at Indiana University. I never had a journalism class. Yet I'm on radio and television every day. My career took off in the direction it did because I started out as an advocate for things that mattered to me.

6. You've got to be of service to other people.

....

7. Be a pioneer. There are too many issues for us to tackle for anyone to claim they can't make a contribution.

8. Don't covet other people's gifts. We often get caught up in "I want to be like this person." Everyone is gifted in different ways. Do what you can do; don't worry about what someone else brings to the table.

9. Doing what's right is not about competing with other people. We live in a world that seems to be based upon competition. That is not what advocacy is about. Compete only with yourself. How can I be a better person?

10. If we fail to explore what our talents are, we'll never know what we might have made of ourselves. Going back to the parable, that one gift the person hid in the earth could have been the greatest of all the gifts Jesus gave out that day.

My grandfather used to say some of the best ideas lie in the graveyard. Too many of us go to our graves with all our energy, power, passion, and talent in tow, untapped and unused. Don't let the world go unaware of your talent or gift.

I'd rather live for a cause than live "just because." Each of us has to find something to live for, something to believe in, to fight for. It makes life more fulfilling, more rewarding, to live for something worthwhile rather than just rolling through this world until your number is called.

Are you starting to feel a little revved up? A little like maybe you, too, can make a difference? Good. What I want to do next is to give you the tools you can use to do so.

3

What Are You Waiting For?
Why People Don't Advocate

O n June 15, 1963, President John F. Kennedy sent a telegram to two hundred leading lawyers, summoning them to the White House. "I am meeting with a group of leaders of the bar, to discuss certain aspects of the nation's civil rights problem. This matter merits serious and immediate attention," Kennedy's telegram read. When the president calls saying something like that, you go, and these lawyers did just that. Among them was a young attorney from Philadelphia named Jerome J. Shestack. He paid rapt attention as President

Kennedy, flanked by his brother Attorney General Robert F. Kennedy and Vice President Lyndon Johnson, asked these lawyers to get personally involved in the fight for civil rights. "He said the winds of change are in the air, and the lawyers are helping to make the difference," Shestack recalled recently. "So I went to Mississippi. I got very involved in the civil rights movement."

As a result of Kennedy's call to arms, Shestack and his colleagues used their legal skills to advance the cause of integration in the segregated South. "You couldn't get lawyers in the South to take a case. They would lose their clients. They were afraid they would be ostracized," he says. "But the law helped change the way of life in the South. The law changes custom, custom changes tradition, and tradition changes a way of life, and that's what happened in the South."

For Shestack, it marked the beginning of a lifetime of advocacy for civil rights. He served as the first executive director of the Lawyers Committee for Civil Rights Under Law, the organization that grew out of the meeting Kennedy called. In the late 1970s President Jimmy Carter appointed him an ambassador for human rights, and later he became president of the American Bar Association, insisting during his tenure that minorities constitute 17 percent of his appointments. He devoted at least a third of his billable time working pro bono—that is, for free—on cases

....

rooted in poverty and discrimination. He does so to this day, still practicing law in Philadelphia at an age at which he could be retired.

Shestack and all the lawyers who joined the civil rights movement as a result of Kennedy's call didn't do so simply because they were inspired. They felt in their guts that they were about to jump into a fight they could *win*. That's the way it is in fighting for what you believe in. The easiest fights to become engaged in are those where you think you have a chance at doing some good, of making a lasting change for the better.

When people are reluctant to stand up for what they believe in, it's not because they don't want to be a force for change. It's not because they lack principle. I believe there are several basic reasons why people shy away from being advocates:

1. They don't know how.

While it is increasingly difficult to act with conviction and compassion in such hurried and somewhat cynical times, I believe most people don't advocate simply because they don't know how! They don't know where to start. Indeed, many of us don't trust our own ability to make a difference, and so we conclude that our advocacy isn't really worth the cost of getting involved. We decry certain social, political, and economic ills, but we leave the work for others to do, fearing that we are not up to the task, that we don't have the ability to make a difference.

People turn away from tackling certain issues because they appear too tough, too complex, or too far removed from their realities. They think they have to wait for the ideal time to act. Well, there is no perfect time. As Bill Cosby once told me, if you're always talking about writing a book, at some point you have to just stop talking and do it, or else you never will.

The truth is, according to Paul Rogat Loeb, a scholar at Seattle's Center for Ethical Leadership, "there are no natural leaders or followers, no people who by virtue of superior genetic traits, become activists." Innately, none of us really knows how to fight for what we believe in. We find our way to making a difference through imperfect processes. Advocacy is like any other thing in life that we do without a blueprint or formula, such as raising our children or caring for our parents as they grow old.

Most advocates are out there feeling their way. There have been times when I wasn't sure about what I was doing, where I needed to find my way. But I learned it was far more important not to procrastinate, rather than waiting for everything to be just so.

We live in a culture in which goodness is equated with naiveté, where we are trained to cut our losses before we ever learn the hows, whens, or whats. One of advocacy's greatest joys is the process of discovering how it works. Fighting for what you believe can reveal miraculous inner sources of courage and heart. We can never know beforehand what the consequences of our actions might be. But we aren't the only ones out there who do not know exactly what we are doing. Even our greatest leaders, from Cesar Chavez to Lech Walesa, were uncertain about what course to take when they first stood up for what they believe in.

2. They're just too busy

We live in a twenty-four-hour society, where work—and life—seem to intrude around the clock. So while people see their quality of life eroding, as a result of pollution, crime, and social unrest, so often they feel they don't have the time to do something about it. They have to do the grocery shopping. Junior has to be picked up from soccer practice; Suzy has ballet. There is a 7:30 dinner with the boss and we're exhausted after a ten- to fourteen-hour workday. There's no time for aerobics, the PTA, tae-bo, or friends, much less global warming.

But the deteriorating quality of life we complain about so vocally isn't going to right itself magically. The only way to effect change is to take charge. Somehow we've got to shift our priorities, find the time, and put in the sweat equity that will allow us to make a difference.

3. They're disconnected.

Some people want to be involved, but they don't know whom to call. They march into City Hall and don't know whom to talk to. These people may take the steps to figure out what to do or whom to call, but when they do, they get the ol' runaround. They are handed a generic business card or get bumped down a chain of aides. Few things are more discouraging to those who are trying to make a difference than having their enthusiasm and energy banked by bureaucracy.

4. They fear the consequences of action.

Some people don't get involved because they are afraid of committing too much of themselves. They wonder, "What if I get in over my head? What if I'm ostracized by my friends? What if I lose my job? What if my family doesn't support the time commitment involved?"

For those interested in running for office, whether for city council, the school board, or state representative, there are legitimate concerns over raising money and becoming beholden to the interests that finance you. If you're battling corporate malfeasance or corruption in local government, there may be fears of reprisals, or more commonly in our litigious society, a lawsuit.

5. They don't believe anything they do will change things.

As Americans, with a glorious Constitution and Bill of Rights, where the very birth of our nation arose out of the rebellion against the British empire and the Revolutionary War that followed, we have a birthright as agitators. In the protest known as the Boston Tea Party, colonists tossed shipfuls of British tea into the Atlantic Ocean rather than pay higher taxes on it; during the abolitionist movement, people created an Underground Railroad to hide slaves and help them escape to freedom. Yet this country increasingly seems to discourage the activism that is the bedrock of our history and of the freedoms we enjoy. This discouragement often comes in subtle ways, such as friends, colleagues, peers, and loved ones rolling their eyes and sighing, "Here we go again," as you broach an important issue. It is exacerbated when people laugh at you for trying to rally them to a cause. This discouragement eventually hardens into cynicism.

In the past, as people's consciousness was pricked by a cause, they felt compelled to do something about it. Today cynicism freezes us in our tracks, preventing us from acting. People just don't feel their efforts will trickle down

....

to where they can do the most good. Nothing is more defeating than the feeling that nothing you can do will make a bit of difference anyway.

But individuals have to walk together toward a common goal. You *can* be an effective advocate and persuade people to your causes—if you can get over your cynicism, and your fear, and your disconnectedness, and your being too busy, and your not knowing how. One person fighting the good fight can make a difference. And one person joined by another, and another, quickly forms a coalition and, eventually, a movement. We *can* make a difference. Moreover, we *must*.

What are you passionate about? If you're passionate about something, people will listen to what you have to say, even if they don't agree with you. They will give you an ear. I thought Newt Gingrich was as wrong as two left shoes. But Newt Gingrich was so passionate about what he believed that the country had to listen to him. And no one inspired his people, his country, and the world like Nelson Mandela, even as he languished for almost three decades in prison.

I've put together a simple worksheet to help you sort out the issues *you'd* like to take on and tackle. Perhaps there is a cause you feel strongly about but have never taken up; perhaps there is something you've been interested in but you just couldn't find a way to help. By listing the things that stir your passions the most—whether in your community, at work, in the schools, or on matters of national import—you may be able to identify the cause or causes that excite you the most and stir you to get involved.

1. List the issues or concerns that stir your interest or passion and explain why they are important to you.

Issue:_____

It is important to me because:_____

_____

_____

_____

_____

_____

Issue:_____

It is important to me because:_____

_____

_____

_____

_____

_____

....

_____

Issue:_____

It is important to me because:_____

_____

_____

_____

_____

_____

_____

2. List the things you could do to help make a difference in the cause or causes that excite you the most.

Issue:_____

Things I could do:_____

_____

_____

_____

_____

_____

_____

Issue:_____

Things I could do:_____

_____

_____

_____

_____

_____

_____

Issue:_____

Things I could do:_____

_____

_____

_____

_____

_____

_____

Now that you have some idea of the things you might want to involve yourself in, and what you might be able to contribute, it is time to learn how to join the fight.

....

4

Pick Your Hills

My grandmother used to say to me that while there were some battles that are not worth fighting even if you win, there are others that are worth fighting even if you lose. My father, military man that he is, put it more succinctly: "Son, pick your hills." They were both saying, be selective. Choose the fights that really matter, the ones where you think you can be most effective.

I believe that you've got to be fully committed to the causes you advocate, because if not, you're going to find yourself down the road wondering, "How did I get into this?," frantically searching for an exit. Before you throw yourself into a cause, make sure it's one you're passionate about, one for which you're willing to sacrifice. You have to be able to strike a balance between conviction and passion. Conviction is the "knowledge" that the cause you're willing to fight for is just and "righteous." Passion is a stirring, burning, abiding sense that you're right. In other words, conviction is about what you believe. Passion is about what you feel. Conviction is the rationale for action; passion is the catalyst for it.

Let me take affirmative action for an example. As a black man, this is something I feel very strongly about. Conviction tells me that affirmative action is a necessity, the reason a whole lot of people of color are employed. Passion, however, makes me want to do something about it. Affirmative action was meant to correct too many lifetimes of wrongs, and in my mind, trying to take it away now, before it's had even one full generation to work for people of color—my people—is disastrous. If I don't take steps to protect it, a whole generation coming behind me will have fewer opportunities than my generation had. Millions of people will suffer.

When I become passionate about a problem, I immediately want to find a remedy for it. I want to fix it.

In deciding on what it is *you* want to spend your pre-

....

cious time and energy fighting for, ask yourself what it is that you are *passionate* about. What causes you to say, "I'm not putting up with this!" Then ask yourself, "Am I willing to fight for it? How should I expend my energies? Is this worth my investment of time, money, and resources?"

Once you've decided that, there is another step I encourage people to take. Before jumping in, you must—as we say in the black community—check yourself before you wreck yourself. What good does it do to be passionate about a particular cause if you let your passion run amok? Being an advocate is about taking risks. But taking risks without thinking them through is not advocacy—it's carelessness. Ask yourself about the depths of your passion—without being influenced by others. Do you truly care enough about a cause to jump fully into the fight for it?

Let's run through that process here. Think about an issue or cause that stirs up the fire in you. When you talk about it, do you raise your voice? I mean, really get loud? Do you experience strong emotion—anger, sorrow, joy—when you talk about it or hear something about it? Do you want to see it changed *now*? Are you sick and tired of the present situation? All of these are indicators of your passion, which will motivate you to act.

Now take your self-examination deeper:

....

★ ★ ★

- Where does this issue fall among the things that matter to you? How high up do you put it on your list of priorities?

- Are you willing to do *something* for it, but only within reason? Is this an issue that is time sensitive—tied to an election or some other specific time frame? If it is ongoing, will you stick with it to the end, through bad breaks and setbacks? Even if it makes you wanna holler?

Conviction is one thing, commitment is another. Think of the great leaders of American history. They don't stand out solely because they acted on their convictions. They stand out because they remained committed to the actions they took. Abraham Lincoln did not give up on the idea of a truly United States, even at the darkest moments of the Civil War. Franklin Delano Roosevelt clung to the notion of full employment, through the darkest days of the Great Depression, and today we have a huge middle class because of it. Martin Luther King, Jr., insisted that his people be freed from the isolation of racial segregation, even as he realized he would not live to see it, and we all now live day to day beside each other because of what he did.

• Are you willing to be challenged, embarrassed, even publicly humiliated by your opponents for this cause? Once you step out, you will encounter challenges and embarrassments as surely as you are alive.

When I worked for Tom Bradley, my job was to ensure that the city responded to people's needs and concerns (and, in the nature of politics, to make the mayor look good to his constituents). I found that responding to people's needs has a tendency to make you welcome and popular. But when I shifted into social and political commentary, how I was perceived by others sometimes underwent a 180-degree about-face. Along with greater popularity came a lot of hate mail. People would stop me in the streets to tell me I was flat-out wrong about this or that. I confronted a great deal of anger and disagreement, and it slapped me against the wall. I was accustomed to being seen as a nice guy, trying to make people happy on behalf of Tom Bradley. I wasn't used to being seen as a troublemaker, an instigator, an enemy. But I discovered that some people out there did see me that way. What I learned from this is that when you become an advocate, you sometimes exchange popularity for hostility. It is conviction and passion that hold you steady in the face of such difficulties.

• Are you willing to make a scene? Cause a stink? Shake, rabble, and rouse? If you plan to be on the front lines, as opposed to helping out in more of a support role, you will be operating on the cutting edge of change. You must be willing to step outside the box, be willing to holler to be heard.

Of course, some folks in this country take the concept of making a scene too far: activists from People for the Ethical Treatment of Animals who throw red paint on the fur coats of strangers to make a statement about animal rights; Act-Up activists who stop traffic in Manhattan to promote awareness of AIDS issues; "tree huggers" who chain themselves to majestic oaks or soaring pines to keep bulldozers from cutting them down; the antiabortionists—or pro-lifers—who issue death threats to abortion doctors, or even go one step further and carry out those threats.

Activism can be an effective tool for change, but these groups hurt other in the process and end up damaging their own credibility. Civil disobedience can have its place. But such social and political drama is better put to use if you make just enough of a scene to get your point across without infringing on the rights of others.

....

• Would you go to jail for what you believe in if you had to? Would you be willing to die for what you believe?

King said a man who has not found something for which he is willing to die is not fit to live. And of course, King did just that—he paid for his advocacy with his life. In the 1960s students staged sit-ins for civil rights and to protest the Vietnam War, and in the 1980s many tried to force sanctions against South Africa over apartheid. Some were clubbed, handcuffed, and marched off to jail. Such issues raise questions: How committed are you? Where do you draw the line? Could you endure six months in prison? A year? Five years? Nelson Mandela languished in prison for twenty-seven years because of what he believed in. His burning desire to see his people free sustained him and ultimately helped him become the first black president of South Africa.

I ask these questions to make you aware of the risks of advocacy; to help you calculate those risks and to gauge your own commitment, conviction, passion. When you can answer these questions to your satisfaction, you know you have a cause worth fighting for.

In times of war, armies do not arbitrarily decide when or how they're going to take a hill. But once they go about trying to take a hill, they do not go about it halfheartedly. Similarly, once you've picked a cause that matters to you,

you want to throw yourself into it with energy. But you have to be aware of the hazards. They're often hidden, like land mines.

Here are some obstacles to avoid.

1. The paralysis of analysis.

Jesse Jackson warned us against this years ago. I love Jesse. Everything he says rhymes, and this particular statement is really, really true. Yes, you want to do your homework, you want to know what you're talking about (I'll discuss this in detail in the next chapter). In other words, you want to be smart about what you're doing. But you don't want to second-guess yourself so much that you can't *act*. There is an overabundance of analysis on many of the issues that galvanize the country. A lot of this analysis is driven by the desire to do what's right and the desire not to do anything wrong. We live in a country where people tend to want to study a problem to death. The answer to too many problems seems to be to appoint a blue-ribbon commission to "look into" it and "report back" to whoever's in charge with "findings" and "recommendations." All of this instead of simply assigning someone to go out and solve the problem.

Recently, President Clinton instructed federal agencies to compile data on whether federal law enforcement officers use "racial profiling" in detaining or arresting people.

He said he wanted to know how often racial profiling takes place. So right now there are people throughout the federal government counting the number of times federal officers, from the National Park Service police to the FBI, come across a person of color while they are out fighting crime. Now, everybody in this country acknowledges police brutality exists. The evidence is not hard to find, from the Rodney King case in Los Angeles to the Abner Louima case in New York City to the statistics on people of color arriving in jail beaten and bruised. Yet police departments and police unions around the country continue to "study the problem" while denying that it exists.

It would have been simpler for President Clinton to say, "If you're a federal officer and you're out there deliberately stopping people from driving, from walking, or from barbecuing in designated picnic areas of Yosemite National Park because they are black, *cut it out*. It's against the law." While such a statement, even from the president, is not the whole answer, it sends a powerful message and it sure avoids the temptation to study and analyze the problem to death.

It's not like we don't know racism remains an omnipresent, divisive issue in this country. Or that people of color continue to lag behind in every economic indicator in this country. Or that discrimination in the workplace

....

still exists. Yet somewhere in America at this very minute, somebody is addressing those problems by appointing another blue-ribbon commission to study them. C'mon, people. The verdict is in on many of the issues that confront us today. We need, as the saying goes, to *plan our work and work our plan*. We can no longer afford to get so bogged down in measuring the dimensions of the problem, and communicating our understanding of it, that we can't focus on a solution.

For some, this paralysis is a deliberate strategy, akin to planting land mines on a battlefield to delay or hold off an advancing army. It prevents people from getting close to the problem at hand. It makes people tread cautiously. This is where conviction and passion are essential.

2. Giving in and giving up.

The Bible says, "Let us not be weary in well doing: for in due season we shall reap, if we faint not." In a fight, you must pace yourself and avoid exhaustion. You can't realistically expect to charge a hill at full speed and make it to the top. You've got to scope out the size of the challenge before you start climbing the hill. Sir Edmund Hillary knew how difficult climbing Mount Everest would be before he set foot on it. There is no better time to find out how difficult the climb will be before you get halfway up.

Otherwise, you may find yourself giving in to fatigue and abandoning the climb. Remember, when you succeed, more likely than not it will be against the odds.

In Chapter 2 I mentioned my political campaign for the Los Angeles City Council. I ran because I felt the incumbent was ineffective and I felt I could do a better job. I asked myself, "Why should I sit around and complain when I could put my hat in the ring and run?" So I did, without realizing what I'd gotten myself into. I had no idea that the campaign would put me through so many ups and downs. One minute I was on the phone collecting cash from contributors, and an hour later I had to deal with the latest poll saying I was trailing and lacked support. Just as I would pick up a key endorsement, I'd find out that one of the local newspapers had endorsed my opponent. Not understanding the scope and magnitude of what you're dealing with can cause you to fail to pace yourself properly. Those who are least weary in the end often win.

3. Lack of vision.

"Where there is no vision, the people perish," the Bible states. *Someone* has to envision a way to make things better. I tell folks all the time if nobody's told you that you're crazy, that your head is in the clouds, then your vision ain't big enough yet. It's only when somebody steps forward to tear you down that you realize you're on the right track.

....

There's something I call the 2/12 rule about working with people. When you get twelve people together, you can count on at least two of them to be a waste of time. Jesus had twelve disciples. Peter denied Jesus three times before the cock crowed, and we all know what Judas did. You, too, are going to have your naysayers. Motivational speaker Les Brown calls them "toxic people." You can't take a hill toting a bunch of toxins around with you!

I can't begin to tell you the number of people who said we would be unsuccessful trying to bring the sitcom *Living Single* and the police drama *New York Undercover* back into Fox's fall lineup. It is generally accepted in Hollywood that once a show has been put on ice, it's virtually impossible to get it back on air. But I thought it was time for the paradigm to shift because those shows were the top two shows watched by African Americans. So I ignored the naysayers. And we won.

Having vision isn't everything. But without vision, you're flying blind.

4. The doubts.

Some people have a very dark view of the world. They don't believe in the basic goodness of people, and they question even the best people's motives. It's very easy to be jaded in today's world, but you can't be an effective advocate if you can't wipe some of that cynicism away and trust

in the basic goodness of people, in their ability to distin-
guish between good and bad, right and wrong. What is life
without hope? It is easy to go from true believer to
doubter when someone disparages your efforts. Invariably,
once you've sized up the hill you are climbing and have
begun making progress, something or someone will ob-
struct your way. Setbacks can make you feel uncertain.
Doubts begin to set in. This is not the time to listen to the
doubting Thomases of the world—and there are a lot of
them—for they will only articulate your fears and make
you believe you can't accomplish your goal.

The campaign to secure a Congressional Gold Medal
for Rosa Parks seemed to me a no-brainer. How could we
not give the nation's highest civilian honor to the eighty-
six-year-old mother of the civil rights movement?
Watching President Clinton's State of the Union address in
January 1999, I saw the entire Congress, as well as Supreme
Court justices and members of the cabinet, give Mrs. Parks
one of the loudest, longest standing ovations I'd ever heard.
Yet a month later Representative Julia Carson called me to
report that HR573, the bill she introduced to get that
medal for Mrs. Parks, was stalled. There were only forty
cosponsors. So I went on the radio and started talking
about the bill. I juxtaposed the televised images of that rare
and wonderful tribute to Mrs. Parks with the fact that by
February—Black History Month, no less—the same

....

members of Congress hadn't signed their names to that resolution. In response, some of these men and women in Congress came to their senses. But as the weeks wore on, I became doubtful about our process. The House minority leader, Dick Gephardt, a Democrat, wasn't on board. Neither was Senator Richard Shelby, a Democrat-turned-Republican from Alabama, the state where Mrs. Parks made history. I never expected to have to ride herd over an issue as simple, as obvious, as honoring Rosa Parks.

I started identifying the holdout members of Congress by name during my radio commentaries and gave out their phone numbers as well. Listeners jammed their phone lines. Their aides would call to cuss at me. Some of the reasons the holdouts gave for not signing just didn't make sense. Ultimately, it took six weeks to get enough signatures.

But I learned something important from this experience. The lack of an immediate response to an issue doesn't mean people are necessarily disinterested or turned off. You've got to keep massaging the process. As the old folks say, being delayed ain't being denied. But you sure feel denied when you're caught up in a delay, and that's where doubt can take over if you allow it. In the end, the resolution to honor Mrs. Parks passed on a nearly unanimous vote. Representative Ron Paul of Texas was the only member of Congress who voted against it. Among those at

....

the ceremony honoring Mrs. Parks that June were Strom Thurmond, Dick Armey, the House majority leader, and Tom DeLay, the majority whip. So we did just fine without Paul and Senator Shelby. (Shelby, by the way, didn't show up to vote for the measure.)

5. Anger.

Anger can be a very useful emotion. Many of the most committed advocates in this country got involved with a cause because they were angry. The 1979 abduction and murder of five-year-old Adam Walsh turned his father, John Walsh, into a crime-fighting crusader. Today Walsh encourages millions of Americans to join him in tracking down criminals through his television program, *America's Most Wanted.* Mark Klaass pressed for changes in California laws regarding sex offenders after his twelve-year-old daughter, Polly, was abducted from her bedroom in Petaluma, California and later killed. These two men acted because they were angry. But they controlled that anger and focused it in a constructive way. You can't just sit back in anger, cursing at society, cursing at the politicians, while failing to do anything to improve the situation. Advocacy is not about being bitter—it is about making things better. What separates those who do from those who don't is that the doers take their pain and turn it into power.

When I first started doing commentaries for radio and

....

TV, I would sometimes lose control if a listener or an opponent baited me. This was especially true if someone made a racist remark. I had to learn to rein in my anger and treat these people not as racists, but as people who disagreed with me. I had to learn to make my case in an appropriate, controlled way without getting drawn into a shouting match. I had to realize I was there to win people over, not humiliate them. That's what advocacy is about, trying to right the wrongs. If in your anger you mislabel those wrongs, then you, too, are wrong.

6. Combat fatigue.

We're all familiar with the phrase "The race goes not to the swift nor the battle to the strong, but to he who endureth to the end." That phrase speaks to both staying power and weariness. Typically, weariness comes when a battle has gone on for a long time, or at least longer than expected. Over time, weariness can turn into burnout. When you're tired, you can always take a break and come back when your batteries are recharged. But if you're burned-out, you're spent. Burnout is a sign that the process has beaten you down, usurped all of your energy.

In his book *The Call of Service: A Witness to Idealism,* Robert Coles told how Martin Luther King made a surprising reference to burnout during a conference in 1964: "A lot of us were sitting at a table talking about the subject because we had witnessed it in others and in ourselves. He explained his somewhat startling choice of words this way: 'We have just so much strength in us. If we give and give and give, we have less and less and less—and after a while, at a certain point, we're so weak and worn, we hoist up the flag of surrender. We surrender to the worst side of ourselves, and then we display that to others. We surrender to self-pity and to spite and to morose self-preoccupation. If you want to call it depression or burnout, well, all right. If you want to call it the triumph of sin—when our goodness has been knocked out from under us, well, all right. Whatever we say or think this is arduous duty, doing this kind of work; to live out one's idealism brings with it hazards.'"

It's one thing to tell yourself that the work you are doing is tough and draining as you plunge ahead sizing up the next hill. But it's a whole 'nother thing when your mind, your body, and all your faculties start to tell you through any number of signs, "I need a break." If you work with the homeless and find yourself one day telling them they're lazy and should just get up and get jobs, you probably need a break. If you are increasingly disenchanted with the people or the situations that you are working to change, you probably need to take a break. This is especially so if you begin to feel that no one appreciates all your blood, sweat, and tears. One doesn't engage in advo-

....

cacy for the awards or the appreciation. If you're waiting for applause, you'll be waiting for a long, long time.

Shortly after returning to America from securing the release of the three American soldiers held as prisoners of war in Yugoslavia, Jesse Jackson listed all the people for whom he risked his life, and told me he hadn't gotten so much as a Christmas card from any of them. Appreciation wasn't what motivated him. "You don't do what I do for awards or appreciation," he told me. Nelson Mandela didn't sit in jail for twenty-seven years, working in a rock quarry so long he almost went blind from the dust, so that he could win the Nobel Peace Prize.

When burnout threatens, take a break and reassess the progress you've made. Look at what you have accomplished. Sometimes that alone can get you back into the fight again. Burnout is surrender. If you surrender, you've failed. Do you really want to be a failure? I don't know about you, but I ain't into waving white flags!

7. *Gloom and doom.*

Just as you feel extreme passion about an issue, you can feel extreme disappointment, or even despair. If you put your all into something, you have a lot riding on it. The folks who start out on fire are too often the ones who get burned-out first. You can end up with a greater sense of despair than the homeless, unemployed guy you're trying

....

to help. The best way to avoid "doom and gloom" is to realize that there is no such thing as an intractable situation. There is no problem on which we cannot make progress. Jesus said the poor will always be with us. But he didn't say each one of them must always be poor. There's no condition we can't make better, no issue we cannot advance, no problem we can't solve, no sorrow we cannot soothe, if only we try.

5

Know What You're Talking About

f you've gotten this far into the book, you must be serious about wanting to make a difference. I've found that the first lesson in advocating change is: Know of what you speak, and speak of what you know.

These days, there is almost no excuse for being ignorant of the issues. After all, we live in what is called the Information Age. Bookstores proliferate, often with more published material on hand than some public libraries. Cable television has made it possible to find shows on almost any subject imaginable—politics, shopping, sports, business, history, cooking—twenty-four hours a day. Computers that once conversed only in the mind-jangling languages of COBOL and DOS today engage us with friendly pictures and graphics. The "information super-highway" that was a vague concept in a government policy statement just a few years ago has since evolved into the Internet, which for millions of Americans has become as easy to use as a telephone. Mailing something often requires a phone line rather than the post office—and it now takes minutes, instead of days, to get a response. It is foolish to avoid this technology, because it offers tremendous advantages to those determined to push their views and advance their causes.

Of course, becoming computer-literate is easier said than done. Some people are simply too afraid of technology. They can't handle programming the VCR or the memory functions of a cordless phone, much less hook up a computer to link them to the Internet.

I put off establishing a Web site so long that by the time I got around to it, a stranger had already grabbed my name. Some lady in Ohio claimed my name as a Web site address in every form available: *tavissmiley.net, tavismiley.org, tavissmiley.com*. She offered to sell my name back to me for $70,000. Because she was technologically savvy and I was not, she was able to snatch my name from underneath me, thinking to herself, "I'm gonna get paid."

I took my time establishing a Web site not just because I was busy but because I am a little timid when it comes to technology. It's hard to embrace technology if you don't understand it. It was all around me and I was oblivious to it. Having my name "taken" from me was quite a wake-up call. In the end, I set up a Web site called *tavistalks.com,* and in its first few weeks it became one of the most popular Web sites on the Internet.

Even the president of the United States is a technophobe. At the time he called for the American people to begin acquiring computer skills, he wasn't honing his own. He sheepishly confessed in 1997 that his daughter was far more technologically savvy than he. During her senior year in high school, Chelsea was writing a report on Coptic Christians in Egypt. Clinton decided to help her. He went to a superior source—the White House library—and proudly pulled nine books and other references for her. But in the time it took the president to work the old-fashioned way, Chelsea had found twenty-seven different resources on Coptic Christians through the Internet, in addition to other computer-aided research she'd already done. That shook Clinton out of his technophobic fog. He asked Chelsea for help. In the weeks before she left Washington to attend Stanford University, Chelsea schooled her father on the finer points of sending e-mail. Today, although he's far from becoming an e-mailing fool, Clinton is at least capable of sending notes to his daughter. He even fired off a congratulatory e-mail to that intrepid senior astronaut, John Glenn, aboard the space shuttle.

My point? There's no excuse for allowing fear of technology to get in the way of your being on top of something you care about. We need to overcome our fear.

Of course, President Clinton had a computer available to him when he was ready to embrace the technology. For some of the rest of us, gaining access to a computer is another story. There is a grave disparity between haves and have-nots when it comes to access to technology, and that disparity becomes even more grave when it comes to households of color. This "digital divide" forces us to confront a question: Can we afford to let a lack of access to technology limit our ability to advocate for what we believe in?

If knowledge and information are power, then you become less powerful without access to them. There are plenty of families in America who *could* afford a computer but spend their money on other things. In other words, not having a computer is a choice they've made. Don't put off purchasing a computer when you can afford to buy the latest stereo or a thirty-six-inch television set with surround sound. Remember: A lack of knowledge is often a direct result of the choices you make, of deciding not to obtain the knowledge you need to fight for what you believe in. Don't let the fight for what you believe in slip away because you're unprepared.

Of course, the Internet is not the only option available for gathering information about an issue that interests you. Information is also abundant at colleges and universities, the Library of Congress or National Archives, municipal or state government offices, and the good old public library. At the library, you'll find not only books on the topics you care about; with the librarian's help you can also search on services such as Lexis and Nexis, which could refer you to more newspaper clippings, magazine articles, even court documents.

So let's say you've decided to join the fight to halt a proposed landfill near your community, but all you know about landfills is that they are giant repositories for trash. Well, you could check with your city's sanitation department to learn where the other landfills are. You could check your local newspaper's archives to learn what happened when landfills were proposed for those neighborhoods. You could go to those communities and talk to long-term residents to learn what impact they say the landfill's proximity has had. You could go to the library and, courtesy of a Nexis search, find articles on neighborhoods that sucessfully fought off landfills. You could also search Lexis for information on lawsuits or court rulings in landfill battles. You could contact any number of environmental groups or associations; they would happily give you information on getting organized or joining an existing group in your area. The possibilities are numerous. A similar approach could be taken on any issue, whether it has to do with education or housing or sales taxes. All that's required of you is a little effort, because in most cases, getting information from these sources is free.

However, whether your information comes from the Internet or a television show, the library or the newspaper, it's not useful if you don't consider the source. You must know what to believe and what to question regarding the things you read, see, and hear. You must learn to read, listen, and watch critically.

Reading (Or, How to Study the Competition)

If you're an advocate, if you're passionately moved by a topic, you have a tremendous leg up if you know what the other side is thinking, saying, and doing. Because there is always another side. And they will fight you tooth and nail, whether you are prepared or not. The best way to prepare to fight for what you believe is to read. Perhaps the great-est tactic you can use to help you win your case is to read as much as possible from the other side's point of view. In other words, study your competition. It doesn't pay just to gather information that supports what you already believe. You are already converted. To convince the undecided and uncommitted, you need to know what the other side is thinking.

How can reading material you disagree with—even disdain—help you? It acts as an early warning system. It lets you know what the other side is likely to come at you with. As any military general or football coach can attest, in order to plot your defense, you must be able to anticipate what the offense is going to do. Though my political philosophies lie on the left, it is the material I've read in right-leaning publications that has yielded some of the best commen-taries I've ever delivered. Just engaging material with which I disagreed got my juices flowing, got my brain cells work-ing. For me, reading those right-wing magazines provides a philosophical frame of reference. I don't subscribe to the beliefs I'm reading. But I absorb them, making me better prepared for the fight before I enter it. In war and espi-onage, this is called counterintelligence.

Once you decide to read, you have to know where to find the right things to read. Often I am asked, "How do

....

you come up with all the stuff you talk about?" The answer is, I read everything I can get my hands on. If it piques
my interest, I tuck it away in a "pending" file. A pending
file gives you a place to put information that may come in
handy later, information that may prick your conscience
differently when you read it a second time. Reading also
creates a way to find areas of consensus. When you're dealing with a difficult problem, you can look for areas of potential agreement in what the opposing side says. There
may be some fights you won't have to wage. If you can
agree on a few things up front, you may win more con-
cessions down the line; at the very least it allows you to
focus on the points on which you really disagree. You and
your opponent may be passionate about the issue at stake,
but if your opponent concedes on points two, three, and
eight, and you compromise on points nine and ten, you
can concentrate your efforts and strategy on the few re-
maining points. So, reading is fundamental to any effort to
advocate a fight for change. No, it's beyond fundamental.
It's as essential as breathing and eating.

But remember, just because you read something in print
doesn't mean it is gospel. Some people are natural-born
skeptics. They operate under the assumption that they
should question everything they read or hear. Give skeptics
something to read, and they'll flip it over, poke it, probe it,
smell it, turn it inside out, question it, then form an opin-

ion about it. In other words, they'll investigate everything about it before they'll put their trust in it. This type of skepticism is a healthy thing—particularly in the Information Age, where "conspiracies" sprout up like weeds because of the free-for-all nature of the Internet. It seems as if we've all got at least one friend who fills our e-mail with alarmist information he or she finds on the World Wide Web: warnings about antiperspirants causing breast cancer; about the Postal Service, with the help of a "Congressman Schnell," concocting a way to tax Internet e-mail; about the need to wipe the tops of soda cans before drinking from them because of the wastes left by rats in warehouses. Some e-mail accounts become a dumping ground for other people's paranoia. Whether any of this stuff is true is not the point. The point is that it is being distributed by people who did not seek to ascertain its validity before sending it on.

The natural-born skeptics who receive such e-mails question them. They want to know which scientists did the breast cancer research, when it was done, and where they can get a copy of the full report. They want to know when Congressman Schnell got elected in the first place, because there wasn't one listed in the current congressional directory when they checked it. They check with Coca-Cola or other manufacturers to determine the truth about that investigation into rats in the soda warehouses. They wouldn't stop buying beverages just because of some unsubstantiated story about rats. They dig a little deeper before deciding to abandon Diet Coke. Such people are doing exactly what good advocates do. They double-check what they read, and refuse to accept something as fact just because they found it circulating on the Internet, read it in a magazine, or came across it in a book.

I recall that in 1998, black people all over the country began to panic because someone told them the Voting Rights Act was about to expire. They sat bolt upright in panic, thinking, "Those white people in Congress are trying to take away my right to vote!" What cracked me up about that was, first of all, it wasn't true. Someone somewhere misinterpreted the renewable nature of the Voting Rights Act and figured if Congress had to renew it, they were probably going to let it expire. I talk about this a lot on the lecture circuit. Blacks all across the country were furious that they were going to lose their voting rights, when many of them hadn't exercised that right in years. If only half as many people became alarmed about the fact that most Americans don't use our right to vote, it would make a monumental difference in our communities. Instead, folks wrote and faxed and e-mailed me about the rumor that they were going to lose their right to vote. When they learned it wasn't so, they fell right back into their complacency.

....

Another advantage to reading is that it helps to ensure we don't repeat the failures of the past. Everyone is familiar with the old adage that those who don't know the past are doomed to repeat it. But few people think about the flip side—that you won't repeat the past if you take the time to learn about it. Take the issue of civil rights. People of color are often the ones who must continue to engage in the struggle for civil rights, for human rights, for fairness. Because it is *our* rights that are often on the line. The fact is, people of color tend to serve as America's moral barometer. We tend to scrape the bottom time after time, and when you're down there with your face smashed up against the pavement, you're better able to tell others exactly how hard that pavement is. Our country has now arrived at a point where, for the first time, we have a generation of Americans—the so-called Generation X—coming into positions of leadership, responsibility, and authority without having lived through the civil rights struggle.

That has consequences for everyone. The further the Jewish community gets away from the Holocaust, the more worried the older generation becomes that the young generation won't understand how fiercely Holocaust survivors vow, "Never again." Hispanics, Latinos, Chicanos worry that assimilation will cause their culture, their heritage, to be lost. White people fear that, with their communities becoming more diverse each day, the lifestyle and cultural touchstones they are familiar with will disappear. What will black America look like twenty, thirty, or forty years down the road, when the new generation out front, leading the way, has a limited sense of what the civil rights struggle was all about?

First-grade teachers often tell their students that reading is the most important thing they will ever learn how to do. And it's true. Reading brings the world beyond to you. Increasingly, because we live in a global world, a global society, it is essential that we have an understanding of worlds beyond our own. Reading allows us to connect to other issues, other people, other struggles in lands vastly different from our own, and see the similarities as well as those things that make us unique. How can we expect to move forward in advocating our beliefs if we lack perspective on the feelings and experiences of those who have gone before us? The easiest and fullest way to gain that experience is through reading.

Listening (Both to What's Said and to What's Left Unsaid)

Remember the day President Clinton stood before us on national television and said, "I want you to listen to me. I

....

did not have sexual relations with that woman"? The president admonished us to pay attention, and we did. And because we listened, his words ultimately came back to bite him in the rear. Yet too often we don't listen to what's being said. Perhaps we instinctively don't believe it. Someone once told me to believe none of what I hear and half of what I read. In any event, all of us have, at least once, been accused of being "hard of listening."

What's the point of listening if you can believe little of what you hear? For one thing, listening teaches you to hear what's *not* being said.

No one knows this better than the mothers of the world. Say something to your mother with a certain inflection in your voice, and she'll know immediately that something's wrong. If you say, "Nothing," she'll challenge you. She heard what you *didn't* say. Some people will discuss a problem but won't claim direct ownership of it. But if you're an attuned listener, you'll be able to read between the lines because of what they don't say. That's what listening teaches you to do.

Often it is the act of listening that raises one's antenna. You don't want to blot out what the other person says because it's too different from what you believe. Listen anyway, even if you think you already know what's going to be said. You'd be surprised at what you can learn about your opponent's position.

....

But you must listen to yourself as well. Some people talk without hearing themselves, only to get caught in a contradiction later. Twice a week, when I do live commentaries on *The Tom Joyner Morning Show,* I take along a cassette tape and record what I've said on air. When I go to the gym to work out, or when I return home, I put that tape in my headset and listen to it. I listen to hear what I said and how I sounded. I also listen because people invariably tell me I said something I did not say.

Listening challenges you to get involved and to respond when you know what you are hearing simply isn't true. The fastest-growing medium in the country is talk radio. The people on it—many of them expressing extreme points of view—help listeners formulate opinions about legitimate issues that later they go to the polls and vote on, that they put money behind, that they put energy and effort behind. They take those opinions as gospel. The fact is, there's too much monologue in America and not enough dialogue.

One of the television sitcoms I helped salvage, *Living Single,* had a funny line about this on one of its episodes. As three of the show's four women characters sat at the kitchen table watching television talk shows, Synclaire, the goofy one, said, "I think instead of all these talk shows they should just have a quiet show, where you watch people thinking about things." Sometimes we would all benefit from a lot less talking and a little more listening.

Watching

Once there was a guy called as a witness in a murder case. The prosecutor asked him to tell what he saw. The witness said, "I heard the sound of the gun go off. I wheeled around and saw the deceased grab himself around the waist. I saw blood gushing out. I saw him inhale, exhale, fall to the floor, and die." The prosecutor asked, "Did you *see* the accused shoot the deceased?" He said, "I heard the sound of the gun go off . . ." Told the story again. The prosecutor said, "Did you *see* the accused shoot the deceased?" He started the story again. The judge jumped in. "Did you *see* the accused pull the trigger?" the judge asked. He said, "Your Honor, I told you, I was there, I heard the sound of the gun go off . . ." The judge said, "That's okay. You're dismissed." He told the jury to disregard the testimony of the witness. The witness got up, started walking out of the courtroom, and when his back was to the judge, he yelled out, "Stupid, ignorant old judge!" The judge said, "What? Stop right where you are!" He had the man approach the bench. He said, "I'm about to find you in contempt of court." "For what?" the man asked. The judge said, "You called me a stupid, ignorant old judge." The man said, "Judge, did you *see* me call you a stupid, ignorant old judge?"

Okay, so it's an old joke. The point is, what you see is equally as important as what you hear. Some journalism schools, in fact, instruct budding reporters to go out and practice observance, taking note of conversations they hear and incidents they see. It's important to watch carefully because sometimes the most important clues you can learn come from the other person's expressions or body language, rather than what is said. Watching lets you see what's coming, and if you ain't watching, you may miss what's coming when it hits.

My grandfather used to stand out on the porch, watching. We'd say, "What are you doing?" He'd say, "Storm's coming." He could tell when a storm was coming just by watching the wind blow, the light shift, feeling his trick knee act up. That's what advocates do—read and listen and watch. Sometimes you have to be the one who sounds the alarm, in order to save everyone else from ending up in the ditch. Sometimes you have to be proactive rather than just reactive.

In one of my recent commentaries, I noted that Florida had just become the first state to have a statewide education voucher program. They can now take tax dollars and give that money in scholarships for kids to go to private and parochial schools. They call it "school choice." Now, I don't like vouchers. To me, they undermine and dismantle public education. The danger, as I saw it, was that the Florida program would be used as a blueprint for other states. Every Republican governor in the cou try, I was afraid, would try to pass that kind of voucher legislation. Texas Governor George W. Bush tried unsuccessfully to pass it in his state before the legislature ended so he could use it in his run for president. Governor Tom Ridge in Pennsylvania was up until four o'clock in the morning, arguing, fighting, pleading with the Pennsylvania legislature to pass school choice on a statewide basis. As I saw it, my job was to go on the radio and talk about what the law in Florida meant, and let everyone know that unless we do something about it, "school choice" is going to pass in every state in this country. It all comes down to being watchful, sounding the alarm, letting the people know, and rallying the troops.

I'm sure you all remember the saying "See no evil, hear no evil, speak no evil." Well, that may be valuable advice in some situations, but it is utterly wrong in standing up for what you believe in. Wrongheadedness must be seen in order to be identified. It must be heard in order to understand how it can be defeated. And it must be spoken about in order to let others know what you know. To fight for what you believe, you need your eyes, your ears, and your mouth wide open.

6

Don't Fight Harder, Fight Smarter

Have you ever expended a lot of energy doing something that, in the end, either failed to live up to your expectations or did not work out at all? Have you ever sat down breathless and spent, wondering: "Did I just do all of that for nothing?" If so, it's time to learn to fight smarter.

Insanity has been said to be doing the same thing the same way and expecting a different result. In a way, this chapter is about avoiding insanity. It's about figuring out what works and what doesn't work so you can maximize your effort, your time, and your energy.

Fighting futilely feels like treading water, barely staying afloat when you know you should be swimming strongly toward your destination. Fighting smarter enables you to push beyond the status quo and really effect change.

Here is a list of ways that can help you to fight smarter as you stand up for what you believe in.

1. **Target your audience.** Figure out who your audience is and focus your energy on reaching out to that target audience.

2. **Speak to the people.** Advocacy, in the end, is about people. It is about person-to-person contact. Explain your campaign to them directly, face-to-face. Knock on their doors if you must. Reach out to them in the most direct fashion possible. What isn't particularly effective is passing out flyers randomly at the mall or on the street, or attempting to change people's opinions with a mass mailing or telephone campaign. Such campaigns may have their place as part of a follow-up effort, but it's hard to get others to see your point of view through an impersonal approach alone.

....

3. **Spend money wisely.** Treat your causes like financial investments. If you're operating with funds contributed by others, inform them of how the money is being spent. It will ensure that they continue to support you. If a disproportionate share of your financial resources is consumed by administrative costs, you are probably not spending money wisely. If your advocacy outfit is reliant on technology but lacks the latest equipment, your efforts will ultimately suffer one day because you're not making the necessary capital improvements. Are you still using a mimeograph machine, Dictaphones, or manual typewriters and rotary phones in the Information Age? If so, your money is being spent unwisely. It's important to understand that most advocacy efforts are not flush with cash in the first place. It's a financial struggle. You're constantly trying to stay afloat, so it is terribly important that you not waste critical funds on antiquated equipment or methods.

It makes no sense to throw money around indiscriminately. You are just spinning your wheels. Politics is rife with people who spent a ton of money seeking public office and got exactly nowhere. Texas billionaire H. Ross Perot dipped into his billions and pushed the notion of a third political party right into

....

the middle of the 1992 presidential campaign. He and his Reform Party were the flavor of the moment. Today Perot is still a billionaire, but he is sitting on the perimeter of the party he founded, watching the political rise of people like former pro wrestler Jesse Ventura, because he didn't carry his vision beyond his wallet. Money well spent is a powerful tool. Money misspent is financial confetti.

4. **Persuade—don't rant or browbeat.** To win people over to your point of view, you must treat them and their opinions with reason and respect, and resist the urge to badger or browbeat them. Over-the-top rhetoric isn't going to win over many converts. Even when over-the-top rhetoric works, it only works in the short term. The alarmist Willie Horton rhetoric may have helped the Republican Party elect George Bush to the presidency, but such race-baiting backfired in later years and alienated a good many people the party was trying to win over.

5. **Tell the truth.** Honesty and sincerity are always more convincing than lies and exaggerations. Lies only lead to more lies.

....

6. **Listen.** People want to be heard. Hillary Rodham Clinton, before deciding to tell the people of New York what she could do for them in the U.S. Senate, went on a statewide "listening tour" to hear the things that were on the people's minds. Without uttering a word, Mrs. Clinton sent a message to voters that she was open to whatever they had to say. Some people call listening a scam—the trendiest posture on the campaign trail. Listening is what some people call a new phase of political nondiscourse. George W. Bush and Bill Bradley, too, went out there doing the "listening" thing as they considered running for president. Some argue that politicians in particular are supposed to present themselves and lay out their positions on the issues for us. They're supposed to share with us, talk to us, while we do the listening. They say this whole listening phenomenon allows for democratic necessities like leadership, principle, and the disinterested formulation of ideas. My response to these criticisms is simple: The more we listen, the more sense we make when we speak. The most effective leaders are those who know how to listen as well as talk. Think about it: Who wants to be told what to do or how to think?

....

7. **Make it easy.** Do whatever you can to make taking part in your cause as easy and convenient as possible. Schedule your event at the right time, in a central location. Provide lunch or child care if appropriate. Offer transportation. Find ways in which even those with minimal time—but genuine interest—can contribute. You can't inconvenience the people you're trying to reach out to. It's just not sensible.

8. **Create a streamlined, concise message.** Dumping an avalanche of information on people is not an effective way to hold their attention or get your point across. Too many faxes, too many phone calls, makes you a nag, not an advocate. Remember, people are pressed for time; don't make them expend too much time trying to understand what you're talking about.

9. **Be careful about the money you raise.** Don't accept money from people in a way that makes you beholden to them for some commitment you may not be able to keep.

10. **Personalize your letters.** Personalized letters make clear to people that you're talking directly to them. Make the tone of your letter respectful, espe-

....

cially if you are on the opposing side of an issue. Keep your letters concise, no more than one page. Keep them focused on a single topic. Form letters do not work. It's a rather lazy way of doing things. It also implies that you don't care enough about the people to whom you are writing to personalize it. And if you're not that interested in the other person, why should he or she be interested in you? Again, so much of advocacy is about reaching out to other people.

11. **Be flexible.** If the cause for which you are advocating is a long-term struggle, you have to be willing to adapt your message to fit today's audiences. Don't get locked into one way of doing things. And don't address younger people you are appealing to in the same way you address older audiences. Tailor your message slightly to your audience.

When I first hit the lecture circuit, like most folks on the circuit I had one or two good speeches. As my exposure grew, so did demand for me grow on the college lecture circuit. But I had developed my speeches for mature audiences. My target demographic was people aged twenty-five to fifty-four. Now I was being asked to do all these speeches on the college circuit. I didn't have a single speech tailored toward younger audiences. I had to find a way to build rapport with younger people. The first two or three times, I bombed because my message was inflexible. I had to really work hard at crafting a message for younger audiences. I decided to speak to them in the language they understand. I used a bit more humor, some slang, more hip-hop references. I stopped dressing in suits and ties and went for a mock turtle or a blazer for my campus appearances; and the relaxed attire helped my audience to see me as younger too. As an advocate, you get the chance to talk to all kinds of people: rich and poor, urban and rural. It's okay to have just one message—but you've got to have more than one way of delivering it.

What doesn't work is resisting change. Pat Buchanan rose to prominence on the strength of his isolationist rhetoric. Today, even though it is obvious that the nations of the world are becoming increasingly interdependent and economies are now intertwined and global rather than separate and national, Buchanan has resisted addressing these changes. As a result, fewer people are receptive to his isolationist stance. He's still out there fighting for what he believes in, but Pat Buchanan is fighting the hard fight, not the smart fight.

12. **Negotiate and compromise.** A friend of mine, George Forbes, has spent years butting heads with the police department in Cleveland, Ohio, in his capacity as president of the Cleveland NAACP chapter and a former member of the city council there. But in whom did the police find an ally when they wanted to protest Mayor Michael White's decision to grant the Ku Klux Klan permission to change clothes at police headquarters after a march? George Forbes! They were willing to set aside their differences to work toward a common goal. You should always be receptive to an acceptable compromise or alliance that will help you achieve your goal. If either George or the police had refused to work together because of their past differences, they both would have been worse off for it.

13. **Work with the decision makers.** First, try to identify people in positions of authority who care about the issues you care about, who are in sync with you ideologically, and court them as allies in your cause. Next, identify those who may not be totally in sync with you but could help you because of the position they hold. You don't have to win them over entirely in order to find ways in which you might work together in a mutually beneficial

way. Take advantage of friends in high places. Even if you are on opposite sides of an issue, sometimes the best way to get what you're fighting for is to challenge that friend to help you. Stabbing in the dark is rarely effective. Find out who the people are that can help you make a difference, and spend your limited time and resources courting those few individuals.

During President Clinton's visit to South Africa, a reporter asked Congresswoman Maxine Waters about whether she thought President Clinton should issue an official apology for slavery. "I'd rather have an apology from Jesse Helms than Bill Clinton," she said. It certainly would have been a greater victory to get archconservative southern senator Jesse Helms to admit the United States perpetrated an egregious wrong by enslaving Africans. In that sense, Maxine Waters was right. But trying to focus on changing the mind of someone as rigid on this issue as Jesse Helms, when you have a president who is far more amenable to your argument—who is also in a position to issue such an apology—just doesn't make sense. At least President Clinton will be inclined to hear you out.

Let me give you another example of what I mean.

....

Most black folk, by and large, have given up trying to change the views of Supreme Court Justice Clarence Thomas. He just ain't gonna change. If anything, he's become even more conservative. In a span of a few years, he's gone from being lampooned on the cover of *Emerge* magazine as an Uncle Tom with a slave handkerchief on his head to being heralded on the cover of the *Weekly Standard* as "America's leading conservative." I can get as upset or angry as I want over his decisions, but that won't affect how Clarence Thomas thinks or what he does. I stand no chance of winning a fight based on changing Thomas's mind. Instead, one must find a way *around* the Clarence Thomases of the world—the people whose minds you just can't change. Spending all your energy trying to convince a person like Clarence Thomas to change his mind would be a hard fight, not a smart fight.

14. **Take advocacy to a higher level.** As Hillary Clinton has said, often advocacy really is politics with a small "p." There is a thin line between the two, and often people who begin as advocates go on to hold elective office because it provides a vehicle to carry their fights to a higher level. There are several such

examples of people currently serving in Congress. Carolyn McCarthy was elected on the strength of her advocacy for gun control laws after her husband was shot to death aboard a Long Island Railroad commuter train. John Lewis rode his record as a student civil rights activist into a position on the Atlanta city council before moving on to Congress. Kimi Gray became an advocate for public housing tenants nationwide based on her efforts to improve her community in Washington, D.C. Don't refuse to allow your advocacy to grow. Take your fight to the biggest venues you can, where you think you can be effective.

In the 1960s, civil rights advocates encouraged people to publicly protest, almost on the spur of the moment, because passions for the cause ran deep. Today Al Sharpton cannot rely on sheer passion to galvanize marchers to protest police brutality. Sharpton talks up his protests on television several days in advance. Essentially, he assembles his forces before going in. He doesn't just say, "We're going to have a march." He doesn't just go to the nearest copying center and print out a lot of flyers, pass 'em out in Harlem, and hope people will show up. He has to mobilize his "troops" in advance. Now, you may or may not agree with Sharpton's politics or his tactics. But we can all learn a lesson from how carefully he organizes the protests and campaigns he mounts.

Fighting Harder, Fighting Smarter: A History

Perhaps one of the best illustrations of fighting harder, as opposed to fighting smarter, has played out over the past five years between the Republicans in Congress and the Democrat in the White House.

The Republicans fought smarter with the creation of the Contract with America. They had an agenda in 1994, a blueprint for what they were going to do. The Democrats did not. In '94 the Democrats were fighting harder. They were operating with an eye on the big picture, trying to do at once all the things that Americans wanted done: health care reform, welfare reform, and so on. They were fighting harder because they were dealing with things on too large a scale, things that were so massive and overreaching it was hard to accomplish anything. That was a harder fight than bringing in an agenda, and the Democrats paid the price by losing their majority in Congress in the 1994 midterm elections.

In the wake of the elections, President Clinton retreated

indoors for some soul-searching. He came out ready to fight smarter. Somehow he got his hands on a strategy manual from the Reagan White House. He reached right into the Republican brain trust and used their own tactics against them in a standoff that led to not one, but two government shutdowns. President Clinton cleaned the Republicans' clocks with an issue the Republicans had brought to the table: a balanced federal budget. The Republicans fought harder by insisting that the budget couldn't be balanced while still making a serious investment in social programs. Clinton fought smarter by finding a way to do both.

The Republicans then allowed the Democrats to claim Republicans wanted to get rid of Medicare and allow elderly people to "just die and go away." They did not fight back because they had Bob Dole, a senior citizen, as their presidential candidate, and they did not feel they needed to put Dole out front articulating their side of this issue. If they had, most elderly people in America would probably have voted for Dole, saying, "He's a senior citizen just like me and he's supporting what I need right now." Instead, they fought harder with denials that did little to penetrate the national psyche.

By 1998 the Republicans were still fighting harder. Because they had not delivered on their Contract with

America, they relied on investigations and impeachment as an election strategy for retaining control of Congress. The White House went down every one of those points in the Contract with America and whipped the Republicans at their own game. The only thing the Republicans got out of it was a balanced budget agreement—but even there they allowed President Clinton to be the architect of the terms. So they had the agenda—that was a smart thing—but they did not follow through on their agenda, and that was a dumb thing. They expected the country to be so shocked by Clinton's behavior that the voters would kick him—and the Democrats—out of office wholesale. In the end, they were barely able to hang on to their majority.

There are any number of examples of harder/smarter tactics outside of politics too. During the NBA strike, for example, the team owners waged a smarter fight by locking their players out. The NBA players were not nearly as prepared for a long-term strike as they thought they were. Many players did not save money in preparation for a strike and began experiencing hardships. They ended up trying to hold charity events to raise money for millionaire basketball players who were going broke, which did not help their public perception. NBA commissioner David Stern had the upper hand the whole time. In the end the NBA didn't lose much, and the players found themselves doing public service announcements to help the league draw fans back so they could play an abbreviated season and draw their paychecks. The players limited their vision to the short term, while the owners dug in for the long haul. And the owners got what they wanted.

Remember: Fight smarter, not harder.

7

Contributing—Putting Your Two Cents In

I f you've been following the steps I've laid out in the previous chapters, you are well on the way to becoming a more involved, interested member of your neighborhood and community. It all begins with your willingness to stand up for what you believe in. So how can you begin? What is the best way you can contribute? Are you a mobilizer or an organizer? Are you someone with more time than money, or more money than time? Someone with tremendous energy but few contacts, or great contacts but little free time? Are you a good writer? A good

....

mingler? Are you more creative or more analytical? Some folks are just strong and willing workers, and every organization is desperate for such help. Some folks dread the mantle of leadership and are content to follow another's lead; others are leaders or organizers who can help others get things done.

Think about who you are and how *you* might best contribute to an organization or a cause. Turn yourself into a hiring committee of one. Decide in what ways you can best contribute now, and then jump in.

Getting Started

Research. Once you decide upon the issue you want to contribute to, or help fight for, the first thing I would advise you to do—based on a lot of hard-won experience—is to gather more information. Find out everything you can about your topic and the ancillary issues. If you intend to work to create a youth program, research everything you can about existing youth programs, about available money, about local politics, about previous efforts. You want to be fully informed on the opportunities that are already available to youth in your area. Find out who else might be interested in becoming involved—social service agencies, schools, local government, parents' associations. Compile the information you uncover.

Accessing Resources. Make contact with others who are interested in joining your effort, and look for whatever resources they and others can bring to the table, from supplies to money to a commitment of time. Do you need to build an organization? If so, do you have the skills to do so—or do you need to reach out to someone else who does have those skills? Begin to map out a strategy based on the resources—people, time, money—you have available. Do you need more? How much can you reasonably hope to accomplish, given the tools at hand? Finally, establish a goal: What is it you hope to accomplish and in what time frame?

Networking. Networking is about connecting people to resources. Again, the more you are able to reach out to the people who can help you, the more you will be able to accomplish. Not everyone you contact will be able to jump into the trenches with you and fight shoulder-to-shoulder, but they can put you in contact with someone who can help, who knows another person who can help, and so forth. Don't be afraid to recruit an army—even if it's an army of one—to your cause.

Writing Letters. Letters are an effective way of reaching elected officials specifically. If you're writing a member of

....

Congress, don't forget to include the identifying number of the specific bill or bills you're concerned about. If you've voted for the elected official before, don't hesitate to point that out. Always include a contact phone number so you can be reached later. And always, always ask for a meeting.

Writing letters also works for organization heads, company heads, foundations, and anyone else who might help your cause. Letter writing is about accessing the power structure, be it political, economic, or social in nature. And the power structure is always the same. Frederick Douglass said, "Power concedes nothing without a demand. It never has and it never will." It is through letter writing that you can respectfully demand what it is that you want.

One rather contemporary way of advocating through letters is to hire a consultant. Believe it or not, there are consultants who get paid to write letters on behalf of those in advocacy. They get paid in part because people don't know how to do it. If you have the money, that's another option available to you. Most homespun advocates, of course, don't have that kind of cash available. Remember, it's probably to your advantage to write your own letters. A consultant may help you write the letter, but *you* have to go to the meeting, not the consultant.

Arranging a Meeting

Once you've launched your campaign, whether by letter, telephone, fax, or e-mail, and have laid out what it is you want, it's important to try to talk to the person or people involved face-to-face.

In the world of politics, this practice is called lobbying. And lobbying is exactly what it sounds like. You stand in the lobbies of the House, Senate, or some other government building, waiting for the people you want to talk to so you can explain your position and what you want done. At least, that's how it worked in the good old days. Now, of course, in Congress there are a lot of people in those lobbies and hallways with you, looking for various senators and representatives too. But you can incorporate the same tactics in corralling a company spokesperson, city council member, state agency head, or local school board member. What you want to try to do is introduce yourself, show yourself to be a concerned citizen (or voter, consumer, parent), and request a meeting—together, one-on-one—in the immediate future. Undoubtedly, the person will have to check his or her calendar. So follow up later that day or week.

If more than one of you goes to such a meeting, decide on talking points beforehand, who will speak first, and what

....

specific actions you will ask for. Be on time. And be willing to wait if the person you are meeting with is not there when you arrive. If you can't meet the official you wish to see, talk with his or her assistant; assistants are likely to be more knowledgeable on the issue in question anyway. Articulate your concerns quickly, clearly, and concisely, sharing anecdotes if you think they'll be effective. Avoid arguments, and disagree politely. If you're asked about something you don't know, admit it. If you need to come back with further information, do so quickly. Don't try to bluff your way through. It can be pretty embarrassing if you get caught in an inaccuracy. Take notes, and compare them with your colleagues' notes after the meeting. Remember, how you follow up after the meeting may be as important as or more important than the meeting itself.

Establishing a Web Site

A Web site can help level the playing field, putting smaller organizations on par with larger ones. The first step, though, is establishing your Web address. Here are some tips.

1. Don't wait! Your Web domain will become as important as your Social Security number. Registering your Web name costs less than a pair of Nike running shoes!

....

2. Web addresses are registered on a first-come, first-served basis. That's why the Internet has grown at such a fast pace. Just go to *www.networksolutions.com* and follow the instructions.

3. Although ideally you want to register your name when you're ready to set up a Web site, if you're not quite there yet, at least reserve your name before someone else does. It's very easy. You can do it on-line or by phone with a credit card.

4. Once you have reserved your name, you can use it immediately, as part of your e-mail address to reinforce the identity of your company or organization.

5. If your name or the name you want to use is already taken, be creative. Add a dash, use an acronym or a nickname, come up with a catchy phrase that describes what you do. I ultimately settled on *tavistalks.com* because that's what I do: talk.

Reaching Out to the Media

Take it from me—the media can be an incredibly useful tool in making people aware of the issue you are fighting for. Occasionally, there is enough controversy or "news quotient" to your campaign that the media will come to you. But most of you will have the reverse problem—trying to get reporters, editors, and TV producers interested enough to devote airtime or column inches to the march, rally, forum, or topic you are pushing.

Newspeople are always on the move, their time is always at a premium, and efforts to reach them by phone to let them know about an upcoming event, much less interest them in your efforts, can sometimes drag on for days.

You can increase your success with the media dramatically if you take a few simple steps:

1. Get the phone numbers for the city desk at your local newspaper and the producers' desks at the local television stations. Call to let them know what's going on in your community. Don't assume that they're aware of a protest or rally. Contrary to popular belief, they don't always know what's going on in town at any given moment.

2. Introduce yourself to the city editors or producers who staff those desks through various shifts. If you can develop a friendly relationship with them before breaking news occurs, you may be better able to convince them to cover your efforts.

3. Find out which reporters cover the beats that your advocacy work falls under—health care, education, high school sports—and get to know them as well. Take them to lunch if you can; offer to keep them abreast of what's going on.

4. Make sure all of the people above know how to reach you, especially after hours or on weekends. Include contact numbers on every piece of paper you send them.

5. Utilize e-mail. E-mail delivers information right to where reporters need it: on their computer screens.

6. Minimize the legwork. Reporters will be more receptive to your information if you don't require them to jump through hundreds of hoops to get it. It's a lot easier for them to use a written statement than it is to conduct a phone interview. If they want an interview or further information, they will ask for it.

7. Present your information clearly and refer reporters to other sources that can verify your research or back up your point, including think tanks and universities.

8. Be persistent but don't nag. Reporters will cut you off altogether if you badger them.

....

9. If a reporter does not do a story on your efforts right away, don't panic. But do keep him or her updated— he/she might do a story later on.

10. Keep clippings or tapes of the stories done about your cause. Media organizations tend to dispose of records quickly, so you will need to act as your own archiving service. Over time, you might find the media coming to you for background information—a little extra access that never hurts.

Tavis's Tips

Of course, everyone has their own way of doing things. Here are some of the methods I've employed in my advocacy work; maybe they will work for you as well.

1. Phone trees still work.

That's why I've listed it here as No. 1. There is still no better campaign vehicle than a good phone tree—you know, where each person in your organization has a list of people to call and inform about events. The phone tree has even created a spin-off, the fax tree. Phone trees also work to mobilize people on behalf of your cause. Establish a mechanism to contact one person quickly; that person is then responsible for calling others to get things moving fast. It is especially useful if you need to respond to a development in minutes rather than days. Just be sure to keep a current list of phone and fax numbers.

2. Delegate duties according to skill.

If you know someone else is more skilled or talented at a particular task than you are, by all means let that person do it. He or she is not going to undercut you, and your cause may be better advanced because of it. Many an advocate lost a fight by trying to do too much, fearing that he or she would lose the leadership role—and the power inherent in it. Such people try to do everything themselves. Don't let the issue you are fighting for die an unnecessary death.

3. Add personal touches.

Speak from experience when possible. People will relate to you better because they'll have a better sense of who you are. And when they relate to you better, they relate to your cause better. I once underwent knee surgery, at a time when I lacked health insurance. I talked about what that meant in my radio commentaries, and to this day people approach me to ask about my surgery, even though it happened years ago. It was the personal nature of what I said that stuck in their minds.

4. A little laughter never hurts.

People also hear you better when you make them laugh. Whenever you can, inject humor. For example, few people outside of historians and political buffs remember the tobacco debate of the 1996 presidential campaign. But a whole lot of people remember Butt Man, the guy who showed up at campaign rallies dressed as a huge cigarette to lodge his objections to candidates who accepted contributions from cigarette manufacturers. The humor lingers long after the particulars of the issue fade.

5. Focus.

Sometimes we get so excited about a cause that we want to explain everything about it all at once. We want to solve it all at once. In the profusion of detail, it becomes very easy to miss the point. Find one central, specific message and stick with it. You've got to stay on the message. Set priorities on the things that must be done to further your campaign and do them one by one. And make sure your actions are consistent with your message.

6. Keep it simple.

Not everything you do has to be elaborate. I had a debate coach in college who used "Keep It Simple, Make It Plain" as his motto. KISMIP. Get to the point. In your presentations and in your projects, sometimes the things that get your point across the best have the fewest bells and whistles, the least amount of pomp and circumstance. If your message is powerful and convincing, you don't need to dress it up.

7. Never lose sight of the middle.

My friend Geraldo Rivera once gave me this bit of advice, and he should know what he's talking about. Geraldo was once the epitome of everything bad about trash TV. He got his nose broken when one of his "guests" threw a chair, and many remember well his "Capone's vault" fiasco. But Geraldo realized he'd gone too far and managed to push himself back, remold his image, and recapture his credibility by claiming the middle. He made O. J. Simpson the focus of his show on CNBC, articulating how the majority of Americans felt about Simpson. He culminated his makeover by defending President Clinton during the impeachment process. Geraldo's days on the talk show fringe have long since been forgotten and forgiven.

8. Be respectful.

I use the phrase "With all due respect" a lot. But being

....

respectful is more than just a phrase. I want people to know I am respectful of their position even when I disagree with it. You have to have a willingness to respectfully disagree. Listen to others' point of view and then, if you disagree, respond to what they've said. You may not be able to change their minds; but you'll help form the opinions of all those on the sidelines who are evaluating, trying to make up *their* minds. And you'll gain your opponents' respect as well.

9. Always respond.

There may be times that someone is calling or trying to reach you when you don't know who the caller is and why he or she is calling. Always respond to phone calls and correspondence. Don't become so busy or so self-important that you don't take time to do so. This is especially true when your opponent, or somebody you think is on the other side of the issue, calls. For all you know, it may be an opportunity to win a convert. As Yitzhak Rabin said, "You can't make peace with your friends."

10. Share information.

Send both your allies and your enemies articles that make your point. Include a note explaining that you sent the article along because you thought they'd find it interesting. Sign your name to the note to add a personal touch. You'll find that people will respond to you in kind, and you'll make friends even with your opponents. And though they may not change their minds on this issue, they may well join you as an ally on another cause down the road.

11. Notice and make time for young people.

When you convince the young, you're helping to enlist the next generation. Young people can bring incredible amounts of energy and idealism to everything they do. Giving them access and an open ear is an excellent way to groom those who will ultimately carry on with your work.

12. Be dependable.

Show up when you say you'll be there. If you *must* cancel, be honest about the reason or give plenty of advance notice. If you say you'll follow up, do so. In other words, don't make promises you can't fulfill. Rather than impressing people and furthering your cause, you'll only make them angry and end up shooting yourself in the foot.

13. It's not about money.

Never let the money you make—or the money you collect from fund-raisers—become more important than your efforts to advance your cause. Remember, you're advocating for an issue because you believe in the cause. Never let money supersede the mission.

14. Be forgiving.

Sometimes aides or volunteers may not do things exactly as you want them done. They'll make mistakes. Personality conflicts may arise. The stress of the work you are doing may raise tensions. No matter how pressured your situation becomes, remember to be forgiving. After all, often your colleagues-in-arms are volunteering their time and service too; and we're all human.

15. Write down your thoughts and ideas immediately (and store them on your hard drive).

Don't rely upon your memory to retain the idea you came up with or the information you've learned. First, you'll forget some of it, and second, it isn't available for others to access or raise—or expand on—as long as it remains locked between your ears.

16. Don't defend the low ground.

Sometimes you have to concede when your organization has made a mistake. You cannot defend every action in the name of your cause, and you cannot defend things that don't make sense. When you do that, you make your

....

opponents sound more sensible than they are. Inappropriate actions or behavior should never be justified for the sake of the greater good.

17. Listen to your inner voice.

If your gut tells you something isn't right, it's probably not. That inner voice is speaking out of instinct grounded in experience.

18. Never curse your critics.

Benjamin Franklin once said, "Our critics are our friends, for they do show us our faults." Accept *constructive* criticism. Occasionally, our critics seize upon our trials by error and use that against us. Just as we all have what Andy Warhol called fifteen minutes of fame, we also have our fifteen minutes of folly. Accept the criticism, learn from it, and go on.

19. Don't do everything in a hurry.

As Ben Franklin also wrote, haste makes waste. Take your time in what you are doing and do it right. Rushed execution leads to ineffective advocacy.

Once I was so anxious to get an "air advocacy" campaign started that I went on the air with my facts half-right. That created a number of problems for me. I was wrong (and I *hate* being wrong). I was wrong with 7 million people listening. My critics had a field day with it. I had to go back on air and correct myself. While the campaign was ultimately successful, it did miss a beat because of my haste.

20. Be visible.

How will people know you are an advocate for a particular issue, trying to effect change, if they never see you out there doing it? Visibility is essential. The more people know about you and the issues you are espousing, the better people will know where to send resources, donations, volunteers. Those who are invisible rarely get credit or help.

21. Remember names.

Remembering people's names is one of the most effective ways you can network. It says you know the movers and shakers who matter, and care enough to remember who they are. It shows you were paying attention in meeting them. If you continually have to search for the name of a prominent person in your area of advocacy, it implies you haven't really done your homework and begins to throw your work into question across the board.

....

22. Aides, assistants, and deputies are important too.

More often than not, you will find yourself talking to the staffs of key people you are trying to sway, so get acquainted with them. The better you know their staff, the more inroads you will make.

23. Remember that you represent your issue wherever you go.

Bear in mind that any door that opens for you could close firmly behind you if you come across as ill tempered, overbearing, or dishonest to the people you encounter in your work. Not only will they not want to deal with you, but they may decide not to join your efforts in whatever issue you are advocating. Whether you like it or not, you are the most visible representative of the issues you are fighting for. If you come off badly, so do the issues you are advocating. Undoubtedly, there will be days when you're in a bad mood, but you can't let that allow you to act in a way that hurts what you are fighting for.

24. Learn to be a willing—and able—public speaker.

It doesn't hurt to take part in panel discussions, forums, town hall meetings, debates, or community events. They can be excellent platforms to advance your cause. Let people know you are available. Offer yourself up. Practice your

....

speaking skills—or if you have others in your organization who could handle the public speaking with more
effectiveness, hand the ball over to them. It can be a powerful, and cost-effective, way to reach out to new constituents.

8

Go Tell It on the Mountain

t is essential in fighting for what you believe to win public opinion. To successfully fight for what you believe, you've got to win the hearts and minds of a lot of other people. It's easy to be branded a member of the lunatic fringe if you don't. Moreover, if you ignore public opinion, you allow your opponents to capture that rich ground and dictate the terms of the debate.

Even if logic and the facts suggest one thing and the court of public opinion dictates another, it is the court of public opinion that so often ultimately holds sway. O. J.

Simpson is a classic example. Although he was acquitted of murdering his ex-wife, Nicole Brown Simpson, and her friend Ron Goldman, in the minds of a lot of Americans O. J. was guilty, and he has never been able to win a sportscaster job or do any major product advertising since, and he had to fight to retain custody of his children. The point is, public opinion matters. It has the power and potential to propel seemingly impossible causes to victory. The National Rifle Association, for example, spent much of 1999 on the run because of a shift in public opinion over the availability of guns. People began asking why, with all the shootings that were taking place, the NRA was adamant in justifying the need for semiautomatic weapons of mass destruction. In the same way, the public turned on the tobacco industry when we learned about internal memos outlining how the tobacco companies suppressed research that drew a connection between the use of nicotine and cancer. The heads of seven major tobacco companies took an oath before a congressional committee and then got caught lying in their testimony. The power of the tobacco industry will never be the same again.

President Clinton turned the budget shutdowns in 1996 in his favor by forcefully presenting his case before the court of public opinion. As a result, the Republicans were forced to back down.

....

There are several things *you* can do to win public opinion to your side:

1. **Get there first.** You've got to get to the people before anyone else does. Let's say you and I are on opposite sides of an issue, and we both have decided to launch a petition campaign. If I start knocking on doors first, then you come along six weeks later, who do you think is likely to secure the greater number of signatures? Now, getting there first doesn't necessarily mean that the game is over. But it does mean the chances are greater that you can make the more lasting impression.

2. **Define the conditions and parameters.** What do Republicans do better than Democrats? Republicans are better at the rhetoric of position and defining the issues. They painted everyone left of center as representative of the counterculture and were able to make that label stick no matter how loudly the Democrats protested. When you don't define the parameters, others do.

3. **Feed the public a steady diet of data.** You have to give people the evidence they need to make up their minds about a subject. Sending out information about your message is not enough. It may be the third or the thirteenth time before your point truly breaks the public's consciousness. And there's no

better evidence than a solid set of facts, courtesy of studies, surveys, and statistics.

4. **Tell the public what other people think.** Just as studies and statistics work, so, too, do polls. People always like to know if their thinking is in line with everyone else's, or if they are alone out in left field.

5. **Establish a core constituency.** You can't create waves without having a solid group of supporters in the middle. Remember when "the wave" was popular at football games? To start the wave, you had to persuade those in your section to follow you. That section became the core of a ripple that coursed around the entire stadium. Core constituencies work the same way. Having a solid core constituency allows you to branch out and take some risks.

6. **Word of mouth.** There is nothing more powerful than getting others to take up your issue because they heard about it. That's the best advertisement in the world. But it is a double-edged sword. Word of mouth has to be buttressed by a solid media campaign. You want the word of mouth to be positive, not negative.

7. **Capture the center.** The right and left scare many people. The person who captures the center, where most people live, wins. Once you've established your

....

core constituency, capture all that surrounds it too. Eventually, you'll have a majority.

8. **Repetition.** The religious right will take one specific part of its platform and just hammer, hammer, hammer on it, without ever talking about it in any depth. It's annoying but effective. You may grow weary of the point they're hammering on, but you remember it. It sticks in your brain.

9. **Distraction and diversion.** If your opponents are clearly offering the public a load of bunk, you can often win the public over with the real issues. It stops the other side's momentum. By offering a diversion that changes the subject, you can regain control of the debate.

10. **Slogans/visuals.** Just like repetition, a good slogan can carry your cause forward as little else can. Think about some of the most popular causes. They are typically promoted by a good slogan. Remember the antidrug campaign with the egg in a frying pan ("This is your brain. This is your brain on drugs. Any questions?") or the campaign for environmental preservation ("Give a hoot, don't pollute")? Sometimes you can even appropriate a successful advertising campaign for sociopolitical purposes. What politician in the 1980s didn't use that Wendy's slogan "Where's

the beef?" It certainly didn't hurt George Bush in his 1988 presidential campaign.

11. **Always keep the moral high ground.** Who in our history was the best at this? Dr. Martin Luther King, Jr. You can't call people names. You can't make crazy allegations. You must maintain your dignity, or your own stature will be reduced to the level of your opponent. Be levelheaded. Be firm but polite.

12. **Stay on the offensive and set the agenda.** When President Clinton ran his agenda aground in 1994, he simply reached over and appropriated the Republicans' agenda, claiming credit for everything in the Contract with America in his successful 1996 reelection campaign. Shameless, perhaps. But it worked.

Again, the media is an invaluable tool in swaying public opinion. Write opinion editorials for your local newspaper. Do citizen commentaries on your local television station. If your pockets are deep enough, purchase a full-page newspaper ad or buy some TV advertising time. Post editorials on your own Web site or start your own newsletter. Do whatever is necessary to win the minds and hearts of the public.

And don't be afraid to confront your opponents. Some people have a tendency to avoid a fight, to avoid confrontation with the opposition. But the public respects those who are willing to stand up for what they believe in. You don't have to be nasty or hotheaded. Being firm and polite will take you further. But you have to find a way to win public opinion.

9

Never Give Up

ever give up. Let me repeat that. *Never* give up.
Easy to say, hard to do. But isn't that what life is
all about anyway? Never giving up means you
have a reason to be engaged in the fight. The one way you
guarantee failure is if you stop trying. You've got to believe
in yourself, and what you're fighting for, and persevere.

As you take off on the wings of your enthusiasm, there
are bound to be detractors ready to clip them. The first
thing they'll try to do is keep you in your "place." You

don't understand the issues, they'll say. You're in over your head.

You have to learn to ignore your detractors. You have to tune out their negative thinking with your own positive vision of the cause you're fighting for. Anyone advocating a position in America generally has to answer three basic questions: what, where, and when.

What

What are you passionate about? When answering that question, you must deal with what I call the three Ps: passion, pragmatism, and possibilities. What are the possibilities? What issues can you pragmatically and realistically make a difference on? What are the issues that can be addressed, that *ought* to be addressed right here and right now? Financial advisers urge, when buying stock, that you remember to invest in what you're familiar with. Advocacy is the same way. Ask yourself, "What in my sphere of existence affects me daily?" Are you a parent? Maybe the PTA is your first stop. Are you a woman who has been subjected to abuse, or know of people who were subjected to abuse? Perhaps a women's shelter is an ideal place to make a contribution. Or maybe you lost a family member to cancer and want to work with the American Cancer Society or start a scholarship fund for your loved one. Perhaps you're a young adult trying to figure out just how to make a difference. To young people, I always recommend Public Allies, a member of the AmeriCorps National Service Network. Public Allies identifies a diversity of talented young adults and creates opportunities for them to practice leadership and strengthen their communities in an alliance with people from neighborhoods, nonprofits, business, and government. Respond to what touches you, what impacts you.

What legacy do you want to leave? Yes, I said legacy. When he retired from the Supreme Court, Thurgood Marshall was asked by a reporter how he wanted to be remembered. He replied that he wanted to be remembered as doing the best he could with what he had. Ultimately, he left us a legacy of legal advocacy.

There are all kinds of causes. Animal rights. The rain forests. Homelessness. The Dalai Lama and freedom for Tibet. Right now, the big cause in Hollywood is the repression of women in Afghanistan under the strict Islamic rule of the Taliban. Civil rights. Migrant workers' unions. AIDS research. We've seen most of these movements come to life in our own time. Yet there is so much more to be done. Look at children's rights. While we talk a lot

....

about children being our greatest natural resource and our future, we have yet to establish a full-blown movement around them. That cause is waiting—possibly for you. There are any number of issues like that—issues looking for someone to rally behind them and a place to start.

So when you hear detractors say, "This isn't an issue you should be tackling; it's just not your concern," tell them— and most important, tell yourself—"This is exactly what I need to be doing."

Where

Somebody once said, "Cast down your buckets where you are." Or, as one of my favorite old gospel hymns declares, sometimes we are challenged to brighten the corner where we are. That means you could probably go anyplace to find your advocacy work.

What needs to be done where you are? What cause is waiting, as far away as the other side of town or as close as your own home? Some people think they need to be in a specific place to make a difference, but you can make a difference right where you are. They think they have to travel to Washington, or that the only issues worth taking on are of statewide or national import. They ask, "Where do I go to get started?" I tell them they can start right where they

....

are, right now. It's not about being in a particular place. Anyplace you go in America, people are struggling with the same issues. While you're caught up in deciding where you can make a difference, there are a dozen issues that could benefit from your insight, energy, or attention right now. You don't have to reinvent the wheel. Plenty of organizations need volunteers or an injection of new blood. These organizations are desperate for somebody like you with the energy and charisma to make things happen. So don't get caught up in the trap of finding just the right cause, just the right time, and just the right place. Get to work now on the issues right in front of your face. Get involved. Make a difference.

When detractors imply you should "stay in your place," tell them, "I will, because I can make a difference in any place I stay."

When

The simple answer is right now. Put down the book and pick up a cause. But an equally valid answer is later, when you feel it. I can't definitively tell you when to do something. But you'll know when that moment hits you. When it does, don't pass up the opportunity to act. Don't just say no. Waiting for the ideal time is the excuse of a procrastinator. Don't wait until you have convinced yourself that everything must be just so for you to get involved. Remember, it's not about perfection, it's about passion, it's about purpose.

Just as you must pick your hills, you must decide where and when to begin. Once you do, be dogged and persistent—after all, you know you are doing meaningful work. Remember that change and progress often happen incrementally, not all at once. Don't expect too much too quickly. Keep your goal in mind. It may take sacrifice and struggle to bring your goal to fruition. But very few things that are worthwhile in life come easily.

Remember that in fighting for what you believe in, you are fighting for a better world. You are using your limited time on this earth to make a difference.

By taking some ordinary steps to get involved, you can accomplish extraordinary things and bring about extraordinary results. Each of us must use the unique talents we have all been given to make a contribution, to make our communities, our country, and our world a better place in which to live and work. While it is true that one person cannot do everything, there is *something* for each and every one of us to do, to fight for, to believe in.

I'd like to leave you with a few words passed on to me by my beloved Big Mama:

> *Once a task you have first begun,*
> *Never finish until it is done.*
> *Be the labor great or small,*
> *Do it well or not at all.*

For all of our sakes, do it well, and make a difference.

Advocacy: A Case Study

CompUSA is the nation's largest computer retailer. In 1999 Tom Joyner and I decided to take
on CompUSA because of its pitiful record of advertising on media aimed at African Americans, despite the
fact that black Americans spent an estimated $1.3 billion
on computers and related equipment that year.

The CompUSA campaign was an outcrop of the Katz
Media campaign. Earlier in *Doing What's Right*, we dis-
cussed a Katz Media memo that recommended to Katz's
advertising sales force a practice known as "no urban dic-

tate"—meaning that companies had the right to refuse to advertise on media catering to black or Hispanic audiences, for whatever reason they saw fit. The memo instructed salespeople not to buy time on black or Hispanic radio stations, because clients want to reach "prospects, not suspects," and suggested that black or Hispanic consumers could be reached without spending on such advertising.

At the time, I did a series of searing radio commentaries on *The Tom Joyner Morning Show* stating that this memo was proof of what minorities had been saying for years: that black and Hispanic consumers were paid short shrift. I gave out Katz's phone number to our listeners, and so many people called Katz to complain that the phone system was shut down.

Soon Katz apologized on air.

CompUSA's name was among those companies we'd started watching after the incident with Katz Media. In the year that followed, we hadn't seen any progress in terms of CompUSA responding to black consumers. You can't challenge every company at once, of course; we chose to take on CompUSA because they were the nation's largest computer retailer, and yet their advertising history in black media was abysmal. Clearly there was a "digital divide" between CompUSA's efforts to attract whites and people of color as customers.

I began doing commentaries about CompUSA on the

Tom Joyner show in mid-August 1999. I asked a few simple questions of the company: How much money did CompUSA spend on advertising in black media in the previous fiscal year? How much was being budgeted for the next fiscal year? And what percentage of their overall advertising budget was spent specifically on reaching black consumers?

CompUSA did not respond.

I found their silence puzzling. Katz had responded to us in a matter of days. Two weeks had gone by with no response from CompUSA. I felt they were ignoring us, and decided it was time to come up with a strategy to get their attention. I figured CompUSA executives must have been under the impression that only white men bought computers. What they needed to see in a tangible way, I decided, was that black people across the country spent money in CompUSA stores.

"We need to do something drastic to get their attention," I told our listeners one day. So I asked them to send in to us copies of receipts for products they'd purchased from CompUSA. We would then make up a nice "care" package that we would send to the company headquarters in Dallas.

About four weeks into this process, a letter popped up on Tom's fax machine from someone named Roger Finley, who claimed to be the head of marketing and sales at

CompUSA. The letter was written on CompUSA stationery, and the fax number printed on top, we learned, was within CompUSA's telephone system. This letter was riddled with offensive statements. The one that really riled our listeners insinuated that black-owned businesses were substandard, and suggested that Tom and I would better spend our energy bringing them up to par. I was on vacation at the time, but Tom read parts of this letter on air. Since CompUSA never challenged the letter's authenticity, I referred to it later in a very biting commentary.

Following my commentary, executives from one of CompUSA's advertising agencies called to try to address the concerns we raised. To my shock, they informed me that Roger Finley was not director of marketing and sales; the letter was bogus. I was taken aback. I thought we'd exercised sufficient checks and balances. I went back on air to retract the biting remarks I'd made about the letter—a situation that might well have shipwrecked our campaign. A message coursed through CompUSA's internal e-mail system calling me a shoddy journalist.

I was rattled. Even my personal assistant told me, "You need to get out of this." But as I traveled the country delivering speeches, people would ask, "They're not responding, are they?"—referring to CompUSA—and I had to admit, "No, they're not." It was clear we weren't getting anywhere in our advocacy campaign, despite our efforts.

....

But I realized I couldn't just abandon the campaign. It would have set a terrible precedent. I had taken my listeners halfway down this path, and they were looking to me for leadership. If I turned away, we would have accomplished nothing on this issue or the larger issue of "no urban dictate"; and on any campaign Tom and I launched in the future, companies would assume, "You can wear them down." I just couldn't throw up my hands, saying, "We lost this one."

Sometimes, being backed into a corner can bring you new resolve—and inspire more creative solutions. I decided to take the energy I was putting into thinking about an exit from this campaign and use it to figure out new ways to keep everyone motivated. I went on air to emphasize that the bogus letter did not, in any way, take away from the legitimacy of our campaign.

About two weeks into collecting CompUSA receipts, one of their advertising agency representatives called to tell us they had tried to persuade CompUSA to change their target demographics and expand their reach, and that they thought CompUSA was getting the message. They produced for us a list of urban-formatted radio stations on which CompUSA intended to buy advertising time in the next fiscal year. They also informed us that CompUSA spent 2 percent of their radio budget of $22 million to $25 million on black radio (although not one dime on black publications or television). The agency also presented a list of stations on which CompUSA could advertise to improve that percentage. But the agency went on to tell us that before any of the plans could be put into effect, CompUSA had to cancel all their radio buys because their stock was in free fall.

We were now six weeks into our campaign. The ad agency's representatives asked Tom and me, "What do we need to do to get you guys off CompUSA's back?" We asked them to set up a meeting with CompUSA executives. They ultimately declined to do so. So we kept on collecting receipts. Eventually, we bundled them up in five large boxes and forwarded them to CompUSA headquarters along with a letter requesting that CompUSA President and CEO Jim Halpin meet with us. Once again, CompUSA ignored our request.

By now, eight weeks had elapsed. So I gave out CompUSA's address, phone number, fax number, e-mail—every contact and address available—to our listeners. They began to send messages asking Halpin why his company was ignoring black America. How long did he intend to let that neglect go on? they asked.

Finally, out of pure frustration, I went on air and told listeners CompUSA was engaging in racist behavior. Now I don't throw the *r* word around recklessly. But sometimes things reach a point where ignorance cannot be used as an

....

excuse for inaction, and the only answer appears to be racism. And I had reached that point with CompUSA. I felt the company was just writing off their black consumer base. Would CompUSA have ignored white consumers who had tried as persistently as our listeners had to communicate with them? I told listeners that if CompUSA did not respond by the end of business the following day, we would step up our campaign. I was prepared to give out the direct dials for Halpin, his chief financial officer, the director of marketing and sales, as well as the telephone numbers for several members of CompUSA's board of directors, including their lone black board member. We were beginning to compile information on the company's institutional investors as well.

Meanwhile, CompUSA contacted Dallas Mayor Ron Kirk, who happens to be black, to ask if he would broker an off-the-record meeting with Tom and myself. We refused—we wanted our meeting strictly *on* the record. So CompUSA decided to go through the ABC Radio Network. Tom and I were told by ABC radio executives that CompUSA had threatened a defamation lawsuit.

"Defamation? For what?" we asked. We had simply relayed the facts; didn't we have the right to challenge a corporation or individual that exploited or unfairly treated others? We told ABC we intended to follow through with our campaign. In response, the president of ABC Radio

....

told us that if we didn't hold off on discussing CompUSA until ABC could ascertain whether there were any legitimate grounds for a lawsuit against us, they would pull the plug on Tom's show the next morning—and perhaps for good. We were shocked. Moreover, we had only a few hours to decide what to do. The pressure was enormous. That ABC would attempt to threaten us, and potentially pull the plug on a show that had some 7 million listeners, was incomprehensible to us. The ramifications were enormous, and frankly, I was scared. In a 2 A.M. phone call, Tom and I decided we were on the side of the righteous in this matter—we couldn't back down. After a sleepless night, we decided to proceed, as we informed ABC.

When we went on air the next morning in Dallas, ABC executives were lined up in the studio hallways, staring daggers at Tom as he coolly turned on the microphones and started his broadcast. Throughout the morning, Tom advised listeners that I might be giving my last commentary. You could have cut the tension in the air with a knife.

Finally, in the third hour of the broadcast, I took the mike for my commentary. I had no idea what ABC might do, but I was about to find out. "We did hear from Comp-USA," I told listeners. I went on to describe the threatened lawsuit ABC had informed us of. I paused in my commentary, and asked Tom whether we were still on air. "I think so," he said. So I decided to tell the whole story:

How ABC threatened to pull the plug on *The Tom Joyner Morning Show* if we didn't stop talking about CompUSA. How they tried to make us choose between our careers and our campaign. I said that "Folks might not agree with what we say around here, but they ought to defend our right to say it until the death."

As I uttered the last few words of that commentary—"You don't abridge people's right to free speech"—I felt myself choking up. As I turned off the microphone, tears began to fill my eyes. There was no jocular banter between Tom and me afterward, as there usually is; the studio was completely silent.

That day, listeners flooded ABC phone systems in New York and Dallas, and shut down the phones at Comp-USA. The phone lines in my Los Angeles office and at Black Entertainment Television studios in Washington lit up as well. E-mail about our situation crackled across the Internet, encouraging people to call or write to lodge their complaints.

Tom and I began fielding calls from the national media about ABC's actions, from *The Wall Street Journal, The Atlanta Journal-Constitution, The Washington Post, USA Today, Newsweek,* the Associated Press. It was dizzying. I tried to continue my day as usual, but it was an unusual day.

One of my guests that night on *BET Tonight* was Al

....

Sharpton, whom I had invited on to discuss proposed changes to the so-called 51 percent rule that would lower the ownership percentages used to define what a minority-owned business is, a maneuver some felt could really hurt black companies. Moments after we started our live broadcast, Al said, "I was shocked to wake up this morning to hear the story of how ABC threatened you and Tom Joyner. ABC ought to be ashamed. I'm looking into this. I want you to know if CompUSA does not respond in ten days, I'll be in Dallas to lead a march. We are not going to let people intimidate you and Tom Joyner into silence." I had no idea Al would do that, but I was glad to have the support.

The next morning, Friday, October 15, I was scheduled to fly to St. Louis to address a meeting of black MBAs. As I went through the security check at Washington's National Airport, a few of the security guards broke into applause. "Way to go, Tavis. We are with you," said a female guard holding an electronic wand used for body searches. When I landed in St. Louis and walked toward baggage claim, a shoeshine man came up yelling my name. He'd heard my commentary the day before, he said, and immediately went to a pay phone, found a telephone number for ABC, and called. He didn't get through because the lines were constantly busy. "They'd better be glad I didn't get through, because I wanted to give them a piece of my mind," he told me indignantly.

....

Meanwhile, Tom called my office in Los Angeles looking for me. "Tavis, you'll never guess what happened," he said. CompUSA wanted to meet. On our terms.

When I walked into the ballroom for a speech at Harrah's Casino that evening, people began standing, clapping and cheering wildly. As I took the podium, I told them I appreciated their efforts, and informed them that CompUSA had called and was ready to meet with us. There was more cheering. I realized then that people from all walks of life—from these MBAs to the shoeshine man —were feeling angry, frustrated, aggravated enough over this CompUSA matter to act. And I knew the tide had turned for our campaign.

I flew to Dallas the following day.

Mayor Kirk greeted Tom and me in the lobby of a Dallas office building and escorted us up to a conference room in his law office. Halpin and CompUSA's chief financial officer were waiting—with bodyguards. We shook hands with Halpin and exchanged pleasantries.

"Tavis, how are you? I hate to be meeting under these circumstances, but it's nice to meet you," Halpin said. He took a seat at the head of the table and we settled around him, Tom and I on one side, CompUSA's CFO and Mayor Kirk on the other.

Mayor Kirk proposed that we let Halpin speak first. The mayor said he was certain that once Halpin shared his

....

thoughts, we'd be impressed with what he had to say. "Sure," we said.

Halpin toyed with the paper on his legal pad. He apologized for taking so long to respond to us. Part of the delay, he said, was that he did not know what to do. I looked at Halpin's hands. They were shaking. Then I realized my hands were trembling too. I took my hands off the table, wondering why I was shaking when I felt so calm inside.

For two hours we had a frank, relaxed discussion about the issues. We told Halpin we wanted him to go on air to talk about the situation. At first, Halpin seemed wary. He stepped outside the conference room to discuss his options with his attorneys. The CFO turned to Tom and me, explaining that Halpin suffered at times from stage fright. Outside, Ron Kirk explained to Halpin that neither we nor our listeners would harass or belittle him on air, and Halpin relented.

Halpin agreed to apologize publicly for ignoring our complaints for so long. He said he would consider organizing an internship program for students at historically black colleges. Moreover, he agreed to hire a black advertising agency to do media buys for CompUSA. And on top of that, he promised that listeners who had sent in receipts through our campaign would receive a 10 percent discount on their next purchases in CompUSA stores. As the meeting was ending, Halpin asked for a copy of the bogus Finley letter. He wanted to track down the author. One thing he told us, however, took us completely by surprise. Halpin said his company had never threatened a lawsuit—and he promised to say as much on air.

Tom and I were elated. After ten tension-filled weeks, CompUSA had done a 180-degree turnaround and bowed to our advocacy efforts.

When Halpin came to the studio for the show a few days later, he was met by the ABC radio executives who had threatened to pull Tom's show off the air.

When Halpin came on, he was actually quite funny. He joked that what offended him most was me calling him "ebonically challenged." Then he got down to business and told our audience what he planned to do. He also pledged to hire a Hispanic advertising agency for media buys. That night, Halpin appeared on *BET Tonight* with Tom, by phone. I spoke with Halpin once after that, to thank him for his appearances. He promised to appear on the radio show again to update us on CompUSA's progress.

One thing that impressed me about Halpin during his radio appearance was that he advised any other chief executive who happened to be listening not to ignore black and Hispanic consumers or blindly assume they were reaching out sufficiently to markets of color.

....

We had won an absolute victory. "I can't think of anyone I'd rather share a foxhole with than Tom Joyner and Tavis Smiley," *Time* magazine columnist Jack White wrote about the campaign. "The victory they scored last week by persuading CompUSA Inc., the largest U.S. computer retailer, to dramatically expand its advertising in black-owned media really belongs to the show's 7 million, mostly African-American, listeners. They showed how powerful consumers can be in the fight for racial respect."

A few days later, a BET producer handed me an Associated Press story reporting that American Airlines had decided to hire a black advertising agency to do ads specifically targeting the black community, which the airline called "a vibrant and growing segment" of the American population. The airline said its decision was unprovoked, but the AP story noted that American's action came exactly a week after Halpin's announcement.

"Sometimes the best defense is a good offense," I told listeners the next morning. "I ain't mad at American Airlines! Big ups to the Double-A! I'm not sure they saw the light as much as they felt the heat, but hey, American Airlines is "something special in the air."

I've included the story of our campaign against CompUSA because, in many ways, it ties back to so many

of the lessons I talked about in this book. I had no idea
when we got involved in our CompUSA campaign that
it would take ten weeks to bring about action. I thought
I had sized this "hill" up pretty well, but it was a much
tougher climb than I imagined. But taking on a multinational corporation is more than a passing notion, and is
not for the faint of heart. There were times when I found
myself looking for an exit strategy. But the truth is that
CompUSA's silence wasn't due to the fact that they
didn't care—it was because they were scared and didn't
know how to respond. Halpin was just as nervous and
unsure as Tom and I were. And he was getting advice
from the wrong people. Contrary to what he'd been told,
putting his head in the sand did not make the problem go
away.

As the CompUSA campaign came to an end, I reflected
on the efforts of countless African American listeners from
across the country. As I did, I recalled the words of the late
Oseola McCarty, the poor Mississippi laundress who gave
her entire life's savings for college scholarships for black
students: "If you want to feel proud of yourself, you've got
to do things you can be proud of."

Those tens of thousands who supported the CompUSA
campaign could feel proud of what they had accomplished
because they had done something to be proud of. But

....

more than that, they now had hard evidence of how, even against major multinational corporations, an individual—especially one individual joined to another, who is joined to another—can fight for what he or she believes in and make a difference. We did it, and you can too.

....

ABOUT THE AUTHOR

TAVIS SMILEY is the host of *BET Tonight with Tavis Smiley,* *on Black Entertainment Television,* a live one-hour nightly talk show that reaches 55 million households. In addition, Smiley's political and cultural commentary is heard on *The Tom Joyner Morning Show,* a national radio program with a listenership of 7 million. *The Smiley Report,* his quarterly newsletter, has a circulation of 3 million readers. The author of *Hard Left* and *On Air,* Smiley is one of the most celebrated commentators in America. He divides his time between Washington and Los Angeles.